THE WEDGE EFFECT

Wishes, Education, Drive, Growth, Excellence

How To Overcome The Odds of Being an "At-Risk Youth,"
While Actively Claiming Your Deepest Desires and Wishes In Life

IRIS GONZÁLEZ

Legal Disclaimer

DEDICATED TO…

Ruben Correa, Sr.: Guelo, bendición
Luis Nieves, Jr.: Primo, bendición

ACKNOWLEDGMENTS

First and foremost, thank you to all of my ancestors for guiding and protecting me throughout life, especially in those rough patches.

To my family, especially my (Irish twin) sister Evelyn, brother José, and cousins Atalie, Justin, and Ian, who drive me to go as far as I can in life and show them that their hopes and dreams are possible too.

To my mentors past, present, and future for opening doors, for challenging me, and for always believing in me. The amount of appreciation I have for each of you for investing your time and energy in me is something I am eternally grateful for. I hope you all inspire others to take on a mentoring role.

To the family I have created through the years—friends.

My Smith sisters: Stacy, Rochelle, Krystal, Kim, Nolvia, Tati, Cynthia, Kathy, Michelle, Mirtha, Angélica, Ketura'h, and so many more. I cannot imagine stronger women to surround myself with during undergrad. Each of you are full of grace, strength, and wisdom beyond your years, and I am blessed to have shared that special time with you. I believe we are finding and living through as "Women of the World."

My guiding lights: Suleica and Amanda. Full of patience, compassion, and loyalty, I am blessed to have women like you in my corner.

Abel, Lisa, Alira, Geovanny, Miguel, Jeremy, Steve, Zuly, Aurelis: thank you for providing me with new perspectives, stories, and experiences and for being unapologetically you. Thank you for standing by me and feeding me with endless inspiration, drive, and motivation to continue on.

Thank you to those who are no longer present in my life; I thank you for providing an abundance of teaching moments. Our individual journeys sometimes lead to diverging paths, and that is something that makes life so beautiful.

To my communities—let's continue to build together and bring each other along the way.

CONTENTS

The Transition to Success

W e are not born into success, although some are born with a head start. Every human defines their meaning of success—there is no "one size fits all" or "must-have" list to achieve it. We begin life with our unique set of circumstances that impact our chances of achieving "success". Some factors may include socioeconomic status, physical environment, and resources. Our life "deck of factors" is handed to us at birth, and it makes an impact on our chances of achieving success.

A deeper dive based on my own life and from others that I have grown with and met in different phases of my life shows me that these factors, such as being an inner-city youth or coming from First-Generation families, go hand in hand with these systematic issues that communities like the one I have grown up with face: youth-to-prison pipeline, educational degrees, and workforce opportunities. This "deck of factors" is challenging to combat and makes us vulnerable to becoming victims to these circumstances.

This book, my book, is for people who have grown up with a deck that is challenging to win with. This is for the individuals who were told that they would never amount to anything and that trying was a waste of time. The transition to *my* success is not short or easy. As the first in my family to graduate high school, go to college, join the workforce, and leave everything I knew to pursue my dreams across the country, I have learned that it requires a lot of different things—the hunger to learn, resilience, drive, motivation, courage, and fearlessness.

The most important takeaway is that the road is long and bumpy. There is a long way to go, and it is okay if you are not sure if you are ready. With this book and the information inside it, you will be. Get ready to turn your back on the deck you were dealt, to stop falling prey to excuses, and to stop preventing yourself from going after what you want, and dare to make the life of your dreams.

Some of us have heard "rags to riches" stories with the urban legends about the kid that "got out" and made it big. It was hard for me to believe in any of that when I was younger—after all, there were no role models around me or real people I knew who could say they did it, so why should I believe? That was a driving factor for why I wanted to write this book—to create the example I never had. You can do this. There are many strategies, tips, and techniques you can apply to help you achieve your success.

The WEDGE Effect outlines proven ways of how you can stop letting current circumstances tie you down, complete a 180 degree spin, and start heading in the direction you always wanted to in life. The tools exist, and if you have enough faith and fortitude, I know that you can make it happen. Stick with me because I was once an "at-risk" youth too.

I did not realize I was branded as "at-risk" until I was in high school and ready to start my college application process. I was at a disadvantage to people I had never met, and I had no idea. There were no people I knew that were like those who made it to tell me what was going on at a higher level. All I knew was that I wanted opportunities and experiences that seemed more like fairy tales than possibility. That was okay with me; I had one life to live, and I had to try to go for it, so I rebelled against the system I was born into. I made a full transition from someone earmarked to fail to someone who was living her dreams without limit by the age of 25. Nothing in life can hold you back once you decide to do it.

Join me as I share my story with you on how I rose above my circumstances to being financially secure, successful, and eager to show you how to do the same.

You decide where your fortune lies. Today really can be the beginning of something that will change your life forever. Take the first leap with me and thrive!

WISHES:
DO THEY
COME
TRUE?

CHAPTER 1

Tales of an "At-Risk" Youth

*"Success is not measured by what you accomplish,
but by the opposition you have encountered, and the
courage with which you have maintained the struggle
against overwhelming odds."*
Orison Swett Marden

My name is Iris J. González, and growing up, I was branded an "at-risk" youth. In case you did not know, an at-risk youth is a child who is least likely to transition successfully into an adult who can achieve personal development and economic self-sufficiency. In other words, I belonged to a group of people society classified as not able to support themselves.

In many situations, it felt like I was set up for failure and a constant struggle for survival. I always wanted to show, by action, that this label was set for rejection. I wanted to reject the idea of failure and challenge the idea that we could not win with a losing hand. The key was paying attention to the game of life while holding my hand and making decisions that gave me chances for improving my chances to win. What happened when I did this?

I succeeded.

My Fiery Childhood Years

I was born at the end of a hot Boston summer in 1989 to a teen mom and adult father. I grew up in a second floor apartment off of Uphams Corner and Columbia Road in Dorchester. Eleven months after my arrival came my baby sister, and it was the four of us until my baby brother was born in the spring of 1998.

I grew up in the inner city of Boston in a neighborhood that seemed to always make the nightly news for violence—shootings, stabbings, theft—and was less known for uplifting community moments. Going to sleep to the sounds of screeching tires or ambulance sirens was normal. It was only until I left to college that I realized that the nighttime felt awkwardly silent and hard to sleep to. We lived in a predominant community of color with Cape Verdean and Caribbean neighbors around us that provided an abundance of cultural blends in such a small bubble.

Growing up, my world felt large, but in hindsight, it was so small! I was so numb to my outside environment and had little capacity to focus on it. Life inside the apartment was taking up almost all of my energy. My young mother tried the best she could with the few resources she had, but it was a tough upbringing. My father was a tough soul who always found it challenging to communicate in productive ways. My sister and I made our daily nighttime walk to our parents' room, where we would kiss our parents goodnight and ask for our bendición.

It was like clockwork—my sister and I would get in our beds and start wandering off to dream world. Right before I arrived, I would shake to the screams on the other side of the door. The two voices collided with words that few children should have to hear their parents exchange. I remember the countless times I would tiptoe to the door and crack it open just to see what was happening. I remember walking through the door once, standing in front of both of them, and the transition they made to be mad at me. I learned that there was no stopping them, and this really impacted me as a kid.

As young girls in the home, Mami taught my sister and me foundational skills of order, structure, and cleaning around the house. We were taught to wash dishes, dust, mop, vacuum, do laundry, cook, and other cleaning as fundamentals as growing women in the house who would one day need to keep the home clean for their future husband. My mother was taught these same things at a very young age, and this mentality was normal too. Only later as a teen would I push back and ask why my dad would be fed first, why we would iron his clothes, and why we always seemed to keep the home in order for him. These experiences taught me a lot and helped my independence later on. Mami was teaching my sister and me everything she knew and thought we needed to know in order to survive in this world.

Mami led a very stressful life and was far too young for the pressures that she had to deal with on a daily basis. My grandparents had left her with an aunt and cousins in Puerto Rico when they came to the United States. She went through a lot as a young child in the barrio, living without her parents and feeling like she was a burden in the home, left to cook, clean, and take her cousins' leftovers. My grandparents were trying to transition the family to the United States in order to have better opportunities and chase the "American Dream," and they tried their best to figure out the best strategy to survive and thrive as a family.

My Guela did not have a great role model as a young child either to help her consider the damaging effects leaving my mother in Puerto Rico would have on her in the future. See, Guela was adopted as a very young child in Puerto Rico as my great-grandmother at the time had three children she could not properly care for. My Guela was the oldest, and so she was given up and given to another woman to raise as her own. She recounts the love for the woman who raised her deeply, but even talking to

Guela today, you can hear the child inside and the pain she carries knowing that she was the only one given up. Over the years, Guela has been able to re-establish her relationship with her mother, my bisabuela, and from the outside looking in, you would never know our history.

My mother made it a point to do everything in her power to break the inadvertently vicious cycle our women were passing down to each other through the generations and build our skill set to achieve more. She taught us organization skills, attention to detail, and the value of meeting deadlines. She taught us that we "can achieve anything that we put our minds to" and that education was our only key out. She taught us to rely on nobody to make it happen for us and that independence should be our primary goal. She taught us to be survivors.

My sister and I found school and reading to be our outlets. We would close our door and build fortresses out of blankets. Imagination and creativity kept our minds out of reality. For me, this blossomed into curiosity; I loved taking things apart and putting them back together. Perhaps that was the reason why I fell in love with engineering.

Dealing with Toxic Stress

For a child growing up in rough socio-economic circumstances, there is a real risk that they can be negatively impacted by the effects of toxic stress. When a child constantly has these stressors in their lives without any kind of support base, it impedes their natural development by constantly activating stress response systems in the human body.

This means that the child's ability to learn, behave, and even think[1] normally becomes hampered. There are three kinds of stress responses that exist—positive, tolerable, and toxic. Positive

---

1   Key Concepts, Toxic Stress, http://developingchild.harvard.edu/key_concepts/toxic_stress_response/

stress responses cause a brief increase in heart rate and elevations in hormone levels. A tolerable stress response happens when the body's alert systems are activated to a greater degree.

In this instance, the loss of a loved one, for example, may cause prolonged distress. But with supportive adults in place to help the child adapt, the brain and other organs can recover. A toxic stress response, however, happens when a child is relentlessly exposed to adversity, physical or emotional abuse, or chronic neglect without adequate adult support.

When this happens, it can cause a disruption in brain development and organ infrastructure and improves the chances of contracting stress-related diseases well into their adult years. When stress is triggered from multiple sources, it has a cumulative toll on a human being's mental, physical, and emotional health.

In chaotic or unstable environments where both parents are always struggling to survive in dire financial situations and are perpetually exhausted, toxic stress is common. It is what fuels the cycle of continued poverty and dysfunction through generations. There is now extensive biological research[2] that has proven chronic stress becomes toxic to developing children that have to face poverty, abuse, neglect, neighborhood violence, or mental illnesses from a caregiver.

More and more, early childhood experiences[3] are being understood as some of the most important when it comes to lifelong outcomes. The "early environment" that kids are made to survive in plays a huge role on who they become later on in life. This could be the reason why so many minority groups, such as the Latinos, are branded as "at-risk" youth from birth.

---

2   Carol Gerwin, Pediatricians Take On Toxic Stress, http://developingchild. harvard.edu/resources/stories_from_the_field/tackling_toxic_stress/pediatricians_take_on_toxic_stress/

3   The Effects of Childhood Stress on Health Across the Lifespan, http://www.cdc. gov/ncipc/pub-res/pdf/Childhood_Stress.pdf

Dealing with toxic stress is simple enough—children must have a support system. Evidence shows that even having one supportive parent is enough to negate most of the harmful effects of toxic stress on a child. A child must have the opportunity to develop their executive functions so that self-regulation can develop too.

These skills teach us how to plan, focus our attention, and remember instructions. If, as an adult, you lack these skills because of childhood trauma—**the first step (the very, very first) is to reprogram your brain to improve your executive functions.**

Imagine your brain[4] is an air traffic control system. Right now the planes are crashing, flying in the wrong direction, and causing you daily pain. With the right control over your executive functions, you can run like a modern airport. This is when success becomes possible.

Overcoming Complex Trauma

After reading this, how would you classify your childhood? Did you survive through this? If, like me, you found your childhood to be outside the realm of what children's television suggests it should be, then you may be a victim of complex trauma.[5] There are many types of traumatic stress, and they all take their toll on the developing child.

Defined, complex trauma describes a child's exposure to many prolonged traumatic events and the impact of this consistent exposure on their development. A sequential occurrence of child maltreatment usually triggers this—psychological maltreatment; neglect; physical, emotional, or sexual abuse; and domestic violence that lasts for a long time.

When trauma like this is chronic and happens in the home, emotional dysregulation results as the loss of safety takes over.

---

4   Key Concepts: Executive Function, http://developingchild.harvard.edu/key_concepts/executive_function/

5   Complex Trauma, http://www.nctsnet.org/trauma-types/complex-trauma

Can you recall any toxic stress exposure as a child? Record it here:

_____

_____

_____

_____

_____

_____

_____

_____

This emotional dysregulation often sets off a chain of events that leads to even more trauma in adulthood because the child loses their ability to detect or identify the abusive behavior. They simply adjust and suffer in silence.

The formation of a child's identity is also disrupted, and sometimes they lose the ability to form secure attachments to other people. If you are an adult who suspects that you may have been impacted by complex trauma, then you have a real obstacle in your way. This needs to be dealt with during the course of your recovery so that you can genuinely succeed.

There are long-term health consequences, self-worth issues, cognition trouble, behavior concerns, emotional response hurdles, dissociation, and serious relationship troubles that all stem from complex trauma. In the context of becoming successful, you need to re-learn that you are a powerful human being.

Growing up in a world tainted by violence and uncertainty[6] has trained you to believe that you cannot trust anyone, that the world is an unsafe place, and that you are powerless to change your circumstances. This is simply not true! In order to plan for the future, you need a sense of hope and purpose, the ability to control yourself, and the skill of perceiving other people's actions as being valuable to you.

This is why mindset is one of the most profound ways you can work on changing your circumstances. Overcoming complex trauma will take time and *action*. It is not enough to learn about these principles, but it is necessary to apply them in your daily life as well. This cannot be done without a firm support base of like-minded people.

We define and own our failures. When we fail, we need to look at ourselves first. People own success as well and succeed together. No individual makes it to the top alone. Successful people build together and move forward together, but it took a community to get me where I am today.

Treating complex trauma is a complex business. You need to look into aspects of safety, self-regulation, self-processing, and trauma experience integration so that you can understand why you respond like you do and to consciously change it in the present. It requires ongoing work and the willingness from you to admit when you are wrong.

---

6   Effects of Complex Trauma, http://www.nctsn.org/trauma-types/complex-trauma/effects-of-complex-trauma

> **Can you recall any complex trauma exposure as a child? Record it here:**
>
> _____
>
> _____
>
> _____
>
> _____
>
> _____
>
> _____

Being an "At-Risk" Youth

Imagine living with a label of "at-risk" youth because of circumstances out of your control—a predestined label that you sometimes forget you own and that outsiders seem to always remind you of. It says a lot about the cycle of abuse and poverty. Luckily, you can take this label and completely reject it. I believe that being born into this kind of situation also makes us naturally resilient, and in the long-term, resilience is something many people wish they had.

When your family is poor and every day is a struggle, your focus is on surviving through. You have to grow up a lot quicker, and you can end up harboring a lot more anger (like I did) from your childhood and past circumstances. Not many people are able to recover from that kind of start in life, which is why the label "at-risk" even exists.

Few people make it out of that kind of environment, and even fewer get to create and experience their personal happiness. "Hard times" are not normal times, but kids that have grown up with little else forget that. Being an at-risk youth is a real thing. It is not something that you should be ashamed or embarrassed of. It is something to be proud of and to own, especially when you succeed at overcoming the label. Do not deny where you have come from, for everything impacts your life!

Being a kid who suffered with complex trauma and toxic stress, I was a prime candidate to fail in life. Of course I was! I barely understood what it would be like to not have to struggle every single day. It is easy to get stuck in the quicksand of your circumstances when your mindset has been trained to exist there.

With "at-risk" youth, it is not about "rising above"; it is about "getting unstuck," or the quicksand simply pulls you back down again. From emotional problems, to bad relationships, poor education, problems with authority, and issues regarding our families—our circumstances do not leave us as we become adults. They follow us wherever we go.

Being an "at-risk" youth[7] is like sitting at the poker table of society with a pair of twos. Everyone else has a better hand, and their chances of succeeding are way higher than yours. But you can still win. You can still learn how to get over your trauma and to work on yourself and your life enough to recover so that you can bluff your way to win.

I am not going to sit here and lie to you—it will be hard. But remember, you are no stranger to hardship! Like me, you can learn to channel your life experience into positive things, and you can learn to rediscover yourself as a positive, enlightened human being who is on the path to success instead of following the road to failure.

It begins with a self-assessment. You have to take time to have a hard conversation with yourself and face reality—you cannot

---

7   Janis Kay Dobizl, Understanding At-Risk Youth and Intervention Programs That Help Them Succeed in School, http://www2.uwstout.edu/content/lib/thesis/2002/2002dobizlj.pdf

carry on this way and achieve your goals and aspirations. You need to change and grow in order to give yourself that chance. The definition of insanity is doing the same thing over and over again and expecting different results. But doing what everyone else has been doing around you will only get you as far as they have gotten! Start by being able to identify the problems that you have.

The Truth Behind the Meaning

What does it really mean to be an "at-risk" youth? A lot. You are more at risk for failure than any other demographic that exists. If you ignore this simple fact, you may end up as another statistic without even realizing how it happened. Everyone has their own unique story, but the outcomes are usually the same—failure, drama, struggle, and adversity.

You may already be an adult, in which case you are currently realizing what the term "at-risk" truly meant. Things are harder for you, and you are not quite sure why. If you relate to any of these scenarios, then there is a high chance that you were once an "at-risk" youth.

- *Poverty:* If you grew up poor with parents that constantly struggled to make a living, then there is a good chance you fall into this category. Poverty often begets poverty as kids never learn how to unstick themselves from the cycle. Transitioning into adulthood without a basic financial understanding, education, or job skills is one example.

- *Family instability and dysfunction:* If you grew up with a single parent, one or both abusive parents, or with parents that fought all the time, then you are worse off than many other people. Stable, two-parent homes are associated with better health, academic achievement, and even better social skills. Children exposed to domestic violence, abuse, criminal activity, or substance abuse issues can and will have long-term problems.

- *Minority youth*: If you grew up as a racial minority, then you face many more barriers. White students are less likely to face these barriers, and it gives them a head start in life. Racial discrimination leads to violence and can limit opportunities. Minorities are more likely to live in poverty and have less access to higher quality resources than their white counterparts, which hampers their life progress (e.g., ability to acquire a job or support a family).

- *Schools*: "At-risk" students often attend poorer schools in their neighborhoods, where they receive education more focused on successfully completing tests than true learning. Bullying, gangs, high crime, and low academic outcomes are usually the norm. Your school may have had metal detectors at every chance and uniformed police patrolling your school like mine. These schools lack the resources needed to help these kids get unstuck from the cycles they are in. Poor schooling sets you up for few resources and opportunity for college or university, which limits job opportunities.

These circumstances accumulate and impact each other. Students may be facing challenges in the home that make it difficult to show up in the classroom, or they may be facing bullying at school, which could lead to aggression in the home. With these factors, the combination of outcomes or ways in which this manifests is endless. These situations may lead to students to drop out, having children early on, and/or trapping them into low-paying jobs. There are so many traps for "at-risk" youth that perpetuate the cycle.

When you consider that nearly 40%[8] of kids in the U.S. live in low income families, it is no wonder that there are so many adults that feel like they are trapped in their lives. There is a breakdown

---

8   Youth From Low-Income Families, http://aspe.hhs.gov/hsp/09/vulnerableyouth/3/index.shtml

happening, where youth of color are living in absolute poverty. Racial and ethnic minorities are disproportionally poor compared to the majority. In 2013 alone the poverty rates for African American kids stood at 38.3% and Hispanic kids at 30.4%—with Caucasian children only making up 10.7% of all poor kids in the U.S.

The largest group of poor are Hispanic children at 5.4 million, African American children at 4.2 million, and non-Hispanic Caucasian children at 4.1 million.[9] The good news, however, is that you have the power to change that! You do not have to continue along this dismal road that was paved for you.

What It Means to Be on the Outside

Right now, you are on the outside of society looking in. The reality of your upbringing and situation has caused you to only focus on the small slice of life that you can control. You are easily bogged down in the day-to-day problems of bills, relationships, and your emotional status. You struggle to see the big picture, and as a result, you do not focus on it.

Imagine that life is like a selfie that you want to put on Facebook for the world to see. You have two choices: a really clear photo of your eye or a fuzzy photo of you sitting down. An "at-risk" youth would be drawn to the clear photo of the eye. Sure, it may only be a part of you, but at least it is clear.

The only problem is that no one will know what you look like. Other kids might choose the fuzzy photo of them sitting at a table. It may not be clear, but at least other people can see all of you.

The analogy pertains to life in that "at-risk" youth tend to get bogged down with clear, small details while other children can see the bigger picture because they are not overwhelmed by stress, urgency, and a constant sense of adversity. Being on the outside

9   New Census Data Tell Us That Poverty Fell in 2013, http://www.clasp.org/resources-and-publications/publication-1/2014.09.16-Census-Bureau-Poverty-Data-Report-FINAL.pdf

means being exposed to "at-risk" behaviors[10] like substance abuse, being locked up, dropping out of school, becoming a teen parent, and endless mental health issues such as depression, being abusive, and anger.

These risks are not conducive to a happy, successful life. To break that down on an even more simplistic level, you cannot be successful in life if you continue to be consumed by any of the at-risk behaviors. I used to get caught up in at-risk behaviors, especially as a teenager. I would lie to my mother when I would get home and keep passing along, but none of this was in alignment with doing better for myself.

Right now you may find that you are on the outside of society. There is a way back in! You will need to focus on yourself, your mind, and your level of education if you are going to get it right. But I promise you that with hard work, motivation, and dedication, you can build the kind of successful life for yourself that you have only seen on television before.

The WEDGE Effect: How to Use It

- **You have realized that you are or were once an "at-risk" youth.**
- **You cannot seem to get started or stay on your success path.**
- **You do not know why everything is always such a struggle.**

Now that you understand how much change is ahead of you, let me tell you how the WEDGE Effect can help. I built the system based on a very simple principle.

If you look past your circumstances, you will find a person there. That person wants to succeed more than anything else in their lives despite being crippled by their "at-risk" status. We "at-risk" youths are made of stronger stuff than the average person; we just need to learn to channel that experience in a positive way.

---

10   Randall Grayson, Ph.D., At-Risk Youth & Resilience Factors, http://www.visionrealization.com/Resources/Camper_Devel/At-risk_youth_presentation.pdf

Most people need an open door ahead of them in order to succeed. You know the saying: "When one door closes, another one opens." Well, when you are one of us, all you need is a teeny-tiny wedge in the door, and we can run straight through it. If there is one thing we understand, it is adversity and how to overcome it. That is a strength.

So I have designed this book based on that principle. There are many doors around you right now that lead to success. Some may only be open a crack, while some may be closed. You get to choose which doors to wedge open so that you can burst through them!

To do this you will need to revamp yourself in some exciting ways. I have built WEDGE to help you achieve the desired effect on your life.

- **WEDGE stands for Wishes, Education, Drive, Growth, and Excellence.** If you can work through this sequence, then I am confident that you can achieve success despite your childhood! I know it is true because I have done it.

- **W [Wishes]:** Realize how to move from ideas and desires to action.

- **E [Education]:** Discover why and how you will learn your way to freedom.

- **D [Drive]:** Define your purpose, and learn how self-motivation is a vital tool.

- **G [Growth]:** Determine how you will grow into your dreams.

- **E [Excellence]:** Understand how other people make you successful.

I am confident that by the end of this book you will understand what needs to happen in your daily life in order to correct that damage that occurred from your younger years. There is still time. You are *never* too old to succeed!

It is time to turn the WEDGE Effect on.

The Lives I've Influenced (Interview Spotlight)

This is how people who have helped me succeed describe me as a person. Here you will see their names, ages, and opinions of me to help you better understand my goals with this book.

- *Geovanny Interiano [25, Latino]* A detail-oriented professional with the ability to think "outside of the box." Very determined and focused—a very caring individual who oftentimes takes on the burdens of others. You help, teach, and advocate for people 100%. Often misconstrued, your criticism is very straightforward and honest and is meant to optimize the advice that is being given. Time is very important to you, and those who waste yours don't make it very far in your life. I never have met anyone but you that is the living embodiment of "There is always a way."

- *Zuleika Toribio [24, Dominican]* You are outgoing and hard-working and stop at nothing to accomplish your goals; once you set your mind to it, "it's on." There is nothing or no one who will get in the way of you reaching your goal. You are funny and optimistic. From my first interaction with you, even though it was over the phone, you have challenged me to think outside the "box" and to push myself beyond my normal limits. You have been genuine and sincere even during moments when you've had to be tough and "honest/real."

- *Krystal Cummings [26, Puerto Rican]* What defines Iris most is her love for her family, her Puerto Rican heritage, strength, motivation to succeed, and desire to continue growing.

- *Steve Flores [25, Puerto Rican]* Educated, Puerto Rican, and Proud! Loud and Quiet, Observant, Thoughtful, Progressive, Energetic, Strategist.

- *Cynthia V. Gomez S. [23, Ecuadorian]* You are a perseverant and driven woman who fears no obstacles and encourages change.

- *Leba [25, Dominican]* STRONG willed, outspoken, meticulous, smart, hardworking, kind-hearted, dependable, fragile, honest, mathematical, never gives up, and fun.

- *Michelle Restrepo [26, Colombian]* Vibrant, inspiring, strong willed, warm, and incredibly wise.

- *Stacy Diaz [26, Columbian]* You are frank, articulate, passionate, very intelligent, humorous, uplifting, resilient, and thoughtful.

- *Suly A. [26, Dominican]* I would describe you as focused, goal-oriented, a visionary, intentional, curious, intelligent, passionate, extremely resilient, confident, loving, creative, innovative, hard-core when you need to be, hard worker, sharing—you would give the shirt on your back to a person you love who is in need—you are always striving and looking for better ways you can improve and grow. You are hard as a rock but soft as a marshmallow. You are loyal, honest, trustworthy, and exemplary to those around you.

- *Amanda N. Coats [25, Puerto Rican]* The essence of a person who can evolve. An educated and funny person who can also be very loud and overprotective.

- *Claudine Johnson [Access Counselor]* Intelligent, hardworking, resilient, funny, and an inspiration are a few of the words that I would use to describe Iris. I remember the first time we met, where we began to talk about college and where you would like to attend and your background. I thought to myself how right in front of me was a young woman who was going to do big things in life.

- *Dan Prestegaard [Formerly managed me and is presently a mentor]* Iris is smart, driven, caring, thoughtful, intuitive, and instinctive. She's a driver...but with a heart. She is caring…but gets results. She has a curious mind and a desire to succeed. She has limitless potential, and she will be successful because she has the will to be successful.

- *Evelyn Marie González* Independent, Aggressive, Ambitious, Caring, Loyal, Dedicated, Stubborn

Your Childhood Challenges in Review. These are the things you want to work on:

_____

_____

_____

_____

_____

_____

Take a moment to reflect and summarize:

_____

_____

_____

_____

_____

CHAPTER 2

Understanding Your Wishes

"As a single footstep will not make a path on the earth, so a single thought will not make a pathway in the mind. To make a deep physical path, we walk again and again. To make a deep mental path, we must think over and over the kind of thoughts we wish to dominate our lives."

Henry David Thoreau

A wish can be a powerful thing. It is not just the desire or hope for something that is not easily attainable but the desire that something will happen in our lives that is absent. This is always an opportunity, and I believe that every wish is a gateway to something better.

Growing up with very little makes wishes seem futile, and we begin to believe that they are not the gatekeepers of opportunity, but they are. A wish is the first step on a path that you choose to take, if you have the right tools at your disposal.

Stepping Into Teenage Anarchy

By the time my sister and I entered elementary school, Mami had taught us enough about discipline and learning to excel. We attended Ralph Waldo Emerson Elementary School in Roxbury, full of dreams and wishes for the future. As I got older, my mother tried to find the best possible school to send me to for Advanced Placement in sixth grade, and I ended up attending the Dearborn Middle School in Roxbury. It was not particularly what you would call a "great" school.

I remember high chain fences, concrete grounds, and windows lined with steel to prevent window breakages. There were security systems and metal detectors that would monitor our daily entrance into the school, and police officers were littered around the school at various intervals. It was a school for 11- to 13-year-olds that felt more like a prison than an institution of learning.

With home life becoming harder to deal with as I grew older, attending this school was a major hurdle for me. I often struggled to see the silver lining with so many dark clouds around, but my resolve was unwavering. I was going to get out of there, whatever it took. I would keep my grades up and prove that I belonged somewhere better. It was my greatest wish for a very long time.

I stayed after school studying and preparing for an exam school to help get me into a better public school. It was tiring and draining, and it felt like it was taking the life out of me at 12! One day my hard work paid off. Due to my scores, I was placed in one of Boston's top three public exam schools, called Boston Latin Academy. For grades 7–12, this would be my new home—a place where I could focus on building a future for myself. It was like stepping out of a prison yard and into a fairy tale.

To me, this school felt like a wonderland compared to where I came from. It took a city block and had three floors, our own lockers, an indoor basketball court, and even study periods! There were no more metal detectors or concrete yards. Sure there were still police officers that would patrol, but they seemed more accommodating. I burnt with the desire to excel once again and take myself even further out of these circumstances.

The first few years there I did not perform as my mother

would have liked. I got a few A's but mostly B's, and she was not pleased about this poor performance. She was looking for the straight A's I got as an elementary school student, and I was just not performing. As my inner teenager awoke, my academic focus began to fail. Home had taken its toll on my emotional state.

What Does It Mean to Wish for Something?

Living in a home where verbal abuse was so prominent made me lose parts of myself as a young woman. Like an internal time bomb, those daily reminders of being seen as worthless and useless and that I would never amount to anything had their consequences. I do not think any young person can really get used to hearing these things.

As my mind begged for knowledge, my heart ached for freedom. My home was like a battlefield where I had to defend my mother from the verbal abuse of my father. As a stubborn pre-teen and then teen, I could not sit idly by any longer. Fighting back was the only course of action I had. I learned early to hunker down with my beliefs and see them through.

As a young person facing all of this adversity, wishes became a beacon of hope for me. I wished for better circumstances, I wished for peace at home, and I wished that I could do well enough at school to save my mother, sister, and brother. Those wishes gave me resolve and drove me forward. They were the hope I needed to see the bigger picture.

Many people that are mired in difficult circumstances forget to wish for something better. Reality becomes so hard that these wishes seem futile and childish. However, a wish is the beginning of a process that can change your life. The problem with wishes is that once someone has one, they often keep it secret and hide it away like it is something fragile.

The truth, however, is that a wish is a statement of desire straight from the heart. You do not get anything louder or clearer than a wish, and this is a powerful tool for guidance in your life. When you feel something that deeply inside you, it comes from a place of desperate need. You may have felt it in your darkest moments or your quietest times.

I believe in the strength a person can gain from focusing on a heartfelt wish.[11] You often hear people wanting to change their lives, but they have no idea where to begin. This is when I turn to them and say, if you had three wishes in the world—three personal wishes—what would they be? This helps orientate you in what you really want for yourself.

Once you have located your core wish, you need to think it through. "I wish I was rich" is not a heartfelt wish, because it does not contain any personal details. Instead, try creating a wish that is uniquely personal, and you will see how inspiring it can be. For example, I might tweak the "rich" wish and say, "I wish that by age 27 I have $100,000 in cash to buy myself my first real home because that would make me and my family happy."

You might notice that the wish is very specific and that it runs along a timeline that I have imagined is possible. This wish can then become the center of a plan that I formulate to make this happen for myself. Think of wishes as open-ended questions, not yes or no answers. You will be amazed at what you can achieve when you are being specific, focused, and willing to do whatever it takes to make your wishes a reality.

11   Anna Lemind, How to Make Your Wishes Come True by the Power of Thought, http://www.learning-mind.com/how-to-make-your-wishes-come-true-by-the-power-of-thought/

> **What are your most heartfelt wishes for your life? Record them here:**
>
> _____
>
> _____
>
> _____
>
> _____
>
> _____
>
> _____
>
> _____
>
> _____
>
> _____

The Power of Personal Belief

For me, my wishes stirred something deep inside that wanted to come out. I knew I had the strength to make them happen and that with learning and education, I could find out how to make these wishes a reality. Wishing gave me a strong personal belief in myself that I still hold onto today. I knew what I wanted, and this helped me define who I was as a person.

The tipping point for me came when college began to be a real thing in my life. I was in ninth grade, and I needed to get serious about my future—this was it. While everyone around me fooled around and became trapped in their problems, I wanted to focus on my deepest wishes. And at the time, I wanted to do the unthinkable—I wished to graduate high school.

I would be the first person in my family to make it past the

10th grade and forge a new path ahead for my sister, brother, and cousins. I knew that I could show them that it was possible to make these wishes their reality. All they needed was a personal belief that this was possible. Nothing proves a point better than showing others a wish is possible.

Being a high school graduate was going to be my new normal. In ninth grade I placed myself in Advanced Placement classes, and things got really difficult. I struggled in history and literature class because I could not relate to the faces in the books. Their experiences seemed so foreign, but even though I had no desire to make sense of it all, my wish to graduate kept me focused.

In my mind, I had no choice but to succeed. I would set the example for my family and one day get an amazing scholarship to a college that would teach me how to get unstuck from my current circumstances. I would leave my home issues behind. This was when I learned how powerful wishes[12] really were. When they become beliefs, they can reshape your reality.

I came to discover that everything you really believe in is true. I clung to my wishes so fervently that they became core beliefs. By internalizing them, I managed to make choices in my young years based on these beliefs, and they led me straight out of poverty. It matters what you believe, and too few kids from hard backgrounds believe in themselves.

Belief[13] is something that has been studied by the medical profession, by scientists, and by scholars alike because it has such a profound impact on outcomes. Belief can change medical outcomes, heal people with physical disabilities, and even help people beat fatal illnesses. If there is one thing I can impart in this book, it is that you should never underestimate the power of belief.

12   The Power of Belief, http://www.fragmentsweb.org/fourtx/powbeltx.html
13   Peter W. Halligan, The Power of Belief, http://ukcatalogue.oup.com/product/9780198530107.do

What are your most heartfelt wishes for your life? Record them here:

_____

_____

_____

_____

_____

_____

_____

_____

Now for the hard question—do you believe in yourself? That wish you created earlier—do you honestly believe that you can make it come true? If not, then you lack personal belief. This means that you have work to do to get you to the point where you can stand and say, "Yes! I believe that I can make it happen!"

For me at school, this required additional Advanced Placement classes, hours of study and extra work, and pushing the limits of what everyone around me had achieved. I believed in myself first, and then I did the work to get myself to that level. Then my wish came true. That is how it works!

Changing Your Mindset

Now we reach the real nitty-gritty of wish fulfillment. Surely there is something more to realizing wishes than simply believing in yourself and then putting in the work? You would be right of course. The human mind is a tricky thing, and you should understand how it works in order to get the most out of a heartfelt wish.

This means changing your mindset first and foremost. Belief is an idea that we judge to be true or not true; it can be either positive or negative. Beliefs are directly related to your emotions, and as you know, many of us have confused emotions because of our upbringing. These are the beliefs that you slowly and progressively need to change:

- That you are stuck in your circumstances forever
- That you are helpless to change your life
- That you will never escape the cycle of poverty and struggle
- That you will never be more than what you are right now

Right now, you may believe these things because your past experiences have validated them. Growing up poor and having to face constant adversity and emotional trauma tends to drain hope and fosters the negative belief that "things are how they are." This is simply not true. If it was true, no one would ever be able to unstick themselves from poverty.

Rational judgment dictates that there are two kinds of beliefs to watch out for: confirmation bias,[14] which forces you to pay attention and assign more weight to ideas that support your current beliefs, and disconfirmation bias, which causes you to expend loads of energy trying to disprove ideas that contradict your current belief system.

You need to let go of disconfirmation bias if you are going to succeed. Accuracy with your beliefs is not the goal; validating new beliefs must become the center of attention. It is only by proving something is possible that you eventually believe that it

14   Alex Lickerman, M.D., The Two Kinds of Belief, http://www.psychologytoday. com/blog/happiness-in-world/201104/the-two-kinds-belief

is. Ultimately this boils down to mindset. A negative mindset is constantly trying to disprove beliefs that you reject.

That is why you may wish for a flat screen TV but are never able to actually afford one. You believe that you cannot afford it, so your mindset attempts to prove that is true by taking a passive approach to this wish. You will not work for it, and you may even go out of your way to sabotage any feeble attempts to make it happen—your heart is not in it.

Negative mindsets[15] are fixed and struggle to learn and grow. A positive mindset, on the other hand, is completely different. It recognizes the choice in desire at the heart of your wish. When you choose to be positive, you will prove that something *is* ultimately possible. This aligns your energy with action, and things start to happen.

Now when you wish for that flat screen TV, instead of collapsing into a negative space, you will look for solutions. How can you make it happen? You might need to take on additional work and need to acquire a new skill first. But that positive belief that you can do it is there. Suddenly you find yourself growing, and that flat screen is not far behind!

Learning to Control Your Thoughts

I am going to say it again—what you believe is the truth is, in fact, the truth. Your mind is a powerful weapon and creates the reality that you live in. There is always a choice, even though sometimes that choice is not always apparent. With a negative mindset and constant negative thoughts, you will not grow as a person but shrivel up.

Your mind is like a computer. It learns all the time! So far, it has learned that things are rough in your world. That life is hard and that you need to be on constant alert to get by. You have literally trained your brain to be negative because of your past

---

15 How Can You Change From a Fixed Mindset to a Growth Mindset?, http://mindsetonline.com/changeyourmindset/firststeps/

circumstances. The good news is that you can reclaim control of your thoughts.

All you have to do is be conscious of the way that you think and perceive things. The brain can relearn how to perceive the world with active effort on your part. You can replace those negative thoughts with positive ones and slowly change your perceptions on what is and is not possible. Here is a hint—everything is possible!

Your thoughts are controlling you at the moment, but you can learn to control them. This will be extra hard for you because of your circumstances. "How am I supposed to control my thoughts when I cannot even pay the bills?" you might think. This is a negative thought in itself and totally proves that you are suffering from an ongoing self-sabotage in your thinking.

Ridding yourself of negativity[16] is very liberating. The first thing you need to learn is to let negative thoughts go. A negative thought is often recurrent and bounces around in your head often, driving you into deeper, darker places. Those bills, those bills, those bills—I will never manage! You need to understand that obsessing about something does not change it. It only causes you debilitating emotional stress that makes your situation progressively worse.

When these negative thoughts arrive, you need to usher them out. Catch yourself repeating negative things in your mind, and actively decide to think something positive instead. I *can* cover these bills—I have 10 days. Then allow your mind to progress away from the problem onto solutions. That is the fundamental difference between positive and negative thinking.

Negative thoughts keep you stuck in the same place, while positive thoughts allow you to become creative and inspired and find solutions to your problem. This is the difference between fixed and growth mindsets. Negative thoughts become trapped

---

16 Erika Krull, Depression and Letting Go of Negative Thoughts, http://psychcentral.com/lib/depression-and-letting-go-of-negative-thoughts/0003764

> **What negative thoughts constantly consume your thoughts? Record them here:**
>
> _____
>
> _____
>
> _____
>
> _____
>
> _____
>
> _____
>
> _____
>
> _____

and want to drive you crazy with grief. Positive thoughts invite new information in for healthy thought patterns.

Needless to say, positive thinking requires positive action. If you do not know what the solution could be, you need to find out. I will teach you more about that in a later chapter. For now, you simply need to understand that your thoughts need to be tamed and reclaimed.

Seizing Back Your Destiny

Have you ever heard the phrase "get out of your head!" It may come in those moments when you are being bogged down in negative thinking. Over-analyzing people, places, and experiences causes more emotional trauma to the person stuck in that mindset. Your mind exists to help you get through the day and to help you realize who you are and what you want.

Those feelings do not go away and are hampered by a fault in your thinking system. Growing up "at-risk," for example, can cause your thoughts to veer off the positive path. The constant adversity becomes so much that you have no choice but to snap into survival mode. Due to this, your mind has been focused on surviving instead of fulfilling your destiny.

I believe that everyone in the world has a destiny. We are all different, and each of us has something special and unique to offer the world. What you are drawn to and what makes you happy is a big clue into who you are and what you were meant to do with your life. Do not let your destiny run on autopilot as a product of confused, traumatized thought patterns.

Imagine two identical people starting the same journey in two cars next to each other. The only difference is that one lane is clear and the other is full of obstacles and hazards. As the two cars set out on the journey, the first one pulls ahead with ease—the path is clear! The second, however, becomes knocked, bumped, broken, and punctured with road debris.

The second car eventually loses a tire and a windshield. It becomes dirty and slow and veers off the path. The car keeps going, but it no longer has a destination ahead. The driver is far too busy trying to keep the car moving forward. This is what destiny is like in life. When you face a lot of adversity, it strips you of your ability to stay on track.

You become scarred by things in your life that were less than ideal. You react to negative circumstances and are susceptible to making bad choices. All of these force you to veer off your path. Well, no more! I am here to tell you that hope still exists. There are many pit stops along the way where you can replace your engine and get new tires.

You may still carry the scars of your journey, but you can choose to not let them impact your chosen route. Your destiny is waiting for you, as it always has been. Time is a relentless force that never stops. We are each given an unknown amount of time to achieve what we want in this life. I want to urge you to make the most of your time!

Real happiness is knowing that you are on the right path and heading towards your true destiny. Being unhappy and dissatisfied is a good sign that you have broken down somewhere. **The WEDGE Effect will help you seize back your destiny and reclaim your right to become a successful human being in this world, whatever that means to you.**

It might involve achievement, money, family, or a relationship—only you can discover what real success means in your life. It begins with that wish, a fervent belief, and a sweeping change in mindset. I believe that you can do it. Now it is your turn to believe it too.

Your Realistic Life Wishes in Review: Record them here:

Take a moment to reflect and summarize:

_____

_____

_____

_____

_____

_____

CHAPTER 3

Creating "Active" Desires Right Away

*"Desire is the key to motivation, but it's
determination and commitment to an unrelenting
pursuit of your goal—a commitment to excellence—
that will enable you to attain the success you seek."*
Mario Andretti

The main problem that you might be dealing with right now is the inability to be active about your circumstances. As I have explained, a wish means very little if it cannot be converted into an action. What governs those actions are your thoughts and how you use them in the battle for your realized destiny.

You have come further than most and perhaps survived through some intense trials. I know that you have seen a thing or two. Your experience can be channeled into positive action that can reshape your entire reality. That is why this chapter is on creative active desires and forming the habit of pursuing these desires to their logical conclusions.

Focus Your Mind: Fixing Your Life

If I had two key strengths at school, they were definitely physics and chemistry. I loved understanding how things worked, and solving problems was particularly exciting for me. MySpace had just been released, and mix CDs were all the rage. I taught myself how to code in HTML to tweak my MySpace profile and blow my friends' minds.

I saw opportunity there, and soon I starting earning money for custom layouts; I made mix CDs that I later sold at school for profit. I remember making $45 one day and being in awe of how much money that was. I learned very quickly that it was important to use any and all resources at your disposal to survive. And survive I did!

By the eleventh grade I had made it past my tenth grade goal and had received more education than anyone else in my family. At that point graduating was no longer a goal but a given. My ticket out was college, and I was getting on that train one way or another. At home I fought against the negative thoughts being projected at me—"You will never graduate, and you will end up in jail!" I would never allow that to become my reality.

People and experiences will try to derail your progress, but you have to stay focused despite these obstacles. A few of my friends were getting help with the college process from an organization called Bottom Line. They had counselors who worked one-on-one with you through the application process. I would qualify as a first generation, low-income student.

I met with a woman named Claudine, and the experience changed my life. She was warm and welcoming, a glimpse into my future. It just so happened that this same day, Claudine would use our first meeting as a training opportunity for new counselors that were onboarding as well. I gave her my academic stats, and their jaws dropped. This was the first time a set of adults had ever shown me how impressed they were with me. Claudine immediately approached the founder, Dave, and spoke with him.

"You are going to Smith College," he told me when they returned. I had never heard of the place. It was an all-women's college, and it was where I belonged. Claudine helped me through the entire process, every step of the way. I was accepted at several prestigious institutions, and the only "rejections" I had were from Ivy League schools. Later on I would find out that a labeling myself as "undecided" (and not Engineering) in my application was a large factor into that!

What You Put In...

I will never forget Bottom Line, Claudine, and that application process. She sat with me for weeks organizing selections, writing and editing essays, creating application packages, and dealing with rejections and acceptance letters. I was invited to galas, dinners, and speaking events, and I have to say, I loved every single second of this exposure to this new world.

I was living proof that what you put in is what you get out when it comes to taking action. As I later discovered, we may have a harder time finding resources and opportunities, but it is what you do when you find one (just one is enough) that makes all of the difference. We need the courage to put in the work and reach for those heartfelt desires.

I remember being taken on a custom, free tour of Smith College (provided by Bottom Line and current Bottom Line Smithies), and I fell in love with the idea of going there. Smith would be the place that lifted me out of my home in Boston and took me to a new life of my own design. The long-term vision paid off. With persistence, resilience, and a strong desire to achieve, I was overcoming the odds.

I did it in spite of many rejections and failures that tried to knock me off my path. If I had allowed external factors that I could not control to impact my progress in any way, I could easily have fulfilled my father's prediction and ended up repeating a vicious cycle, filled with anger and regret. However, I did not, because of my desire to be a role model to my family and youth in our community as well as my belief that a childhood wish was possible and outweighed all of it.

For every choice there is a consequence, no matter how young or how old you are. There is no such thing as a passive decision or "letting things just happen." What you do not realize is that inaction is also a choice and therefore an active decision. You need to start seeing your life in this way.

> **Which areas of your life do you think you can put more work into? Record them here:**
>
> _____
>
> _____
>
> _____
>
> _____
>
> _____
>
> _____
>
> _____
>
> _____
>
> _____

Establish a Timescale to Blast Off

To be proactive about your choices is something that is learned; it does not just happen. This is particularly hard with "at-risk" youths because they rarely have adults in their lives that can teach them this virtue. Hard work is not optional in our situations. Even if you are "smart," the underlying premise is that you must also work hard to go far.

No one gets anywhere in life without this hard effort, dedication, and focus in a specific area. To really blast off "ahead of the pack," you will need to learn how to combine this kind of proactive attitude with a timeline. Sure, "time is money," but time can also be other inputs like effort, study, dedication, and a host of other things.

Imagine for a moment that every day you are given a bank account with $86,400.00 in it. This amount does not roll over but expires at the end of the day. How you choose to spend it will determine where you get in life. But here is the kicker: you cannot store the money or buy assets with it—only skills and abilities. There is no cheating to roll over the bank account. In 30 years, the bank closes. What do you do?

What are your thoughts? What do you do? Where should your time be focused?

A resourceful person would spend each and every day looking for innovative ways to invest that $86,400.00. The investment might buy the ability to learn how to start and manage a business or a vital coding skill needed to enter the tech field—the investment is ultimately with you. That is how time works. Every day you are given 86,400 seconds to spend that you can never recover.

In life, we do not know how many years or days we have to invest in ourselves. If we see 30 more, our focus will be on different things than it is today. By then, you need to have made several good decisions about where to invest your time. A good timeline is matched with your ultimate wish or desire and then fueled by hard work. There is no finer equation on earth for succeeding. Face the fact that to succeed you cannot take shortcuts on yourself to get through.

Your Wish = Belief (Truth) + Hard Work + Timeline

Get a new car = What you can afford + saving monthly a targeted goal + hit your target for 6 months

This equation can be used in any context to help take you to a successful result. People that successfully accomplish goals repeatedly know this and put in the time and effort to get it done. People get themselves into trouble when they look for loopholes like get-rich-quick schemes, falling prey to "sounds too good to be true" deals, and other ways to try to create a shortcut. You hurt yourself the most in the end when you take this route.

Without hesitation, time management is a skill that really helps you achieve your successes throughout life—yet it is discounted and sometimes viewed as "not that important" by folks who tend to waste a lot of time thoughtlessly. Are you the kind of person who procrastinates? Wastes time? Ends your day feeling like you accomplished nothing? Then you need to tweak your personal system to create more productivity to achieve success.

Defined, time management[17] is the ability to plan and control how you spend the hours in your day to accomplish your goals. It is a critical element in planning for the future that you will need in your skill arsenal. Do yourself a favor and add "time management" to your list of things that you need to learn about.

Learning How to Build Life Plans

You cannot create successful outcomes without a detailed strategy and plan. Some folks go through their entire lives without a plan or a strategy to help them lead the kind of life that they want and just "go with the flow." Years later, a look back shows that not too much progress has been made on the wishes they have kept in their head. A strategy and plan is a document to work from and focus on. Sure, the plan will not go 100%, and there will be times when you need to adjust—that is fine. What matters is the overall blueprint to work from! With so many roles that a single person has to take on and define, plans can be immensely useful.

Think of a single woman, for example—she may be a mother, a daughter, a sister, a grandmother, an executive, a pet owner, a teacher, a parent, and a loving partner all at the same time to lead the life of her dreams. How can she keep it all together at the same time? A personal life plan helps you reflect and define what success looks and feels like to you. This is the value of starting with a plan.

It is easy for us to derail and get caught in focusing on the wrong things—usually material items like cars, clothes, etc. We should be encouraged to focus on the bigger picture: Where are you going? Where do you want to be? What does your life look and feel like? What experiences have you enjoyed? A solid plan[18]

17 Time Management, http://www.psychologytoday.com/basics/time-management
18 Michael Hyatt, Creating Your Personal Life Plan, http://michaelhyatt.com/creating-your-life-plan

helps give you the framework to get you to where you want to be. It gives you clarity about your purpose and keeps you balanced when obstacles arise and try to knock you off course.

It also gives you peace of mind because you know that you are spending your time valiantly and inching towards the life that you have always dreamed about. A great life plan is a blueprint for the future, nothing more and nothing less. Here is how you can build a basic life plan for yourself in the space of an hour!

- Clearly define all roles that you want to take on in your life. Spend some time describing who you want to be in those roles. Example: Mother (loving, kind, structured, compassionate, fun, trustworthy, reliable, able to provide)

  Pause and consider the roles you want in life. Clearly define them in the space below:

  _____

  _____

  _____

  _____

  _____

  _____

- Next you will want to outline your core goals in life. That means setting an eventual macro goal under each life area and breaking it into micro goals accordingly. Use these to begin: health, career/vocation, financial, intellectual, spiritual, travel, social, and lifestyle.

  Use this space to outline your core goals:

  _____

_____

_____

_____

_____

_____

_____

- Under each life area, create a list of goals that you would like to achieve. Place them under the headings "1 year: short term," "2 years: short term," "5 years: long term," and "10+ years: long term." Work backwards, placing the hardest goals in your long term categories. One-, two-, and five-year plans are great for short-term life orientation.

1 year: short term:

_____

_____

_____

_____

_____

_____

2 years: short term:

_____

_____

_____

_____

_____

_____

_____

5 years: long term:

_____

_____

_____

_____

_____

_____

10 years: long term:

_____

_____

_____

_____

_____

_____

- Once you have organized key goal areas under each heading, you will need to apply adequate timelines to make these goals achievable. Break them down into daily pieces of work or prioritize them by order of importance. Then you can apply actions steps to get you there.

Pause and reflect on the overall exercise from above:

_____

_____

_____

_____

_____

_____

_____

A good life plan document contains where you currently are and where you want to be in two, five, and ten years from the date of creation. It tracks your progress and keeps you on target. It is important to systematically review your goals and year-long plans because they will change as you learn and grow as a person.

My advice would be to search online to find a template for a life plan that suits you. Some are simple and some are complex; decide which best suits your current situation. Always remember, it is never too late to start a life plan!

The Affirmation Station: All Aboard

Hopefully by now you are following along and know that your thoughts create your reality. Now a new question: what creates your thoughts? Language, of course, and how you use it when that inner voice decides to chirp up and assert itself inside your mind. Some people call it the "inner voice" or the "conscious voice," but while this voice acts from past experiences drawn from your subconscious, it can also be influenced and changed by your conscious mind.

That is why I firmly believe in positive self-talk and affirmations. Sure, they seem silly when you begin to use them, but over time the positive effects become apparent. Your mind is like a computer

---

Create five affirmations that combat your five most negative thoughts. Record them here:

1. _____

   _____

2. _____

   _____

3. _____

   _____

4. _____

   _____

5. _____

   _____

---

that has already been programmed. To alter this program, you need to add in fresh lines of code. This will help restructure how you perceive the world.

It is almost a universal thing we do as humans to throw all sorts of self-defeating and negative[19] things at ourselves on a daily basis. Most folks do not realize that this voice is their biggest enemy. An affirmation, simply stated, is a positive statement that is designed to replace an old negative one. If, for example, you are prone to thinking, "I am so fat. I will never lose this weight!' then believe me, you are going to struggle to ever lose it.

This is because you are setting yourself up for failure; it is a self-fulfilling prophecy. Replacing this negative statement with a

---

19 Kate Brit, How to Change Your Mind and Your Life by Using Affirmations, http://tinybuddha.com/blog/how-to-change-your-mind-and-your-life-by-using-affirmations/

positive affirmation means catching yourself wanting to think the negative thing—then forcing yourself to say the positive version either in your mind or out loud several times in front of a mirror. The more you say it, the more your subconscious mind will get the message.

"I am beautiful and love myself fully," for example, or something more proactive like "I am healthier today. I have lost three pounds already. Keep going!" To begin with affirmations, you need to identify the negative ones that are holding you back right now. Write them down on a piece of paper when you experience them

Then, when you have a list, create opposing positive statements that you can use instead. Make a concerted effort to say these positive statements to yourself until they come naturally. You will find that you become happier and more capable because you are not contributing to the adversity and negativity that you have to face every day. This is when inner strength blossoms and grows.

Right now you may be a saboteur of your own life, even without knowing it! You have kept yourself down by convincing yourself that you cannot break out. This is not the truth but instead a reality that you have created and now believe. In order to change that reality, affirmations can give you perspective. In a recent study by Northwestern State University,[20] people that used positive affirmations for two weeks reported a higher self-esteem than at the beginning of the study.

It is time for you to board the affirmation station so that you stop derailing yourself en route to your chosen goals. Even if it feels silly, do it anyway—what have you got to lose?

The Nature of an Active Wish

As I have explained, wishes are very powerful things. They are the first inkling of a desire that comes straight from the heart and

---

20   Using Affirmations, http://www.mindtools.com/pages/article/affirmations.htm

can lead you to new frontiers and happier places. To finalize your education on what wishes can do in your life, I want to tell you about the two kinds of wishes so that you can recognize which one you have.

- An active wish is a wish that is backed up by action and motivation. It usually contains goals and a plan and is set to a specific schedule. When a wish is seen to fruition in this way, you will finally understand how wish fulfillment works. Any wish that is worked on this way will be achieved, guaranteed as long as you never give up.

- A passive wish is a wish that never makes it out of your mind. Because of that, it becomes a taunt or a longing, and you grow bitter that it is something that you will never have. Passive wishes quickly become regrets, especially when they are vivid for the person having them. These need to be turned into active wishes or dumped.

An active wish is a beautiful thing. There are so many benefits when focusing on this kind of wish fulfillment that I could fill several more books with why you should give it a chance. There is a reason why a wish can make dreams come true. Remember in the Disney movies when the princess would wish for something and it would spark a whole adventure?

That is the true nature of an active wish—it is the beginning of a new adventure for you. The first thing you are going to stop doing is using the word "wish" in a negative way: "I wish I had more money" and "I wish I had a better job or worked fewer hours." These negative, passive wishes do not help anyone and serve to bring you down in life.

They have no place in your thoughts, so dispel them immediately! Instead, start using the first step in the WEDGE Effect to empower yourself. W is for wishes. *Active* wishes. Those wishes that are going to change your entire life. You have always been your own fairy godmother, able to make your wildest dreams come true.

If Cinderella really wanted to, she could have sewn her own dress and caught a lift to the party. Destiny is destiny after all, only in the real world, you have to claim it for yourself instead of waiting for some magic windfall to happen to change your life for you. This will never happen—the chances are astronomical!

Begin your journey with:

- I wish…for myself
- I wish…for my significant other
- I wish…for my family
- I wish…for my colleagues
- I wish…for my friends

Then use these amazing fire-starters to motivate yourself to action. If you have been waiting for an invitation to the game of life, then consider this your formal invite. Now what are you going to do with it? An active wish is a happy wish that always comes true.

Realistic Areas in Your Life That Need Hard Work and Timelines:

_____

_____

_____

_____

_____

_____

A Bullet Point Summary of Your Life Plan:

_____

_____

_____

_____

_____

_____

EDUCATION: WHY IS IT SO CRITICAL?

CHAPTER 4

Understanding Why and How to Learn

*"Learn to get in touch with the silence within
yourself, and know that everything in life has
purpose. There are no mistakes, no coincidences, all
events are blessings given to us to learn from."*
Elisabeth Kubler-Ross

Anyone can wish for something that they need in their lives, but after every wish, there is a period of learning that needs to take place in order to fill a knowledge gap. That is why the next step in the WEDGE Effect is Education. We are told that education is something that happens only in school, but this is not the truth.

Education, learning, and gaining new insight and knowledge, are fundamental skills that can and must be harnessed on your road to success. It is not enough to wish for something; you need to know everything about it too. You need to understand how to cross a great divide so that you can become the kind of person who deserves what you want out of life.

The Unchartered College Years

June 2007 was one of the proudest moments in my young life. I was the first person in my family to ever graduate from high school. Even better than that, I had done it so well that I had an amazing college waiting for me—something that had been such a big goal for me over the last 10 years. My focus had never strayed from "getting out"—not once. Later that month, Mami also received her GED, and I was so proud to be her child and share such an amazing achievement with her.

College would be the way I would step out of my personal circumstances and forge a new path for myself and my family. I was most excited to leave my abusive home environment and to go off to explore what life could really offer. I was looking forward to a transformative journey into unraveling my past to become a whole, healthy adult. I felt like I would finally be free of these bonds, and it was the best feeling in the world.

The day my mother drove me out to Northampton, MA, I was only 17 years old, and my world had instantly changed. I said goodbye to my sister, brother, father, and my neighborhood of course—and knew that I had no choice but to make it work on my own. Happiness and excitement flooded through me as I considered what this all meant.

In the end it was bittersweet, and I worried about my sister and brother. I had to leave them behind undefended, but I knew that the only way I could really help them was to leave and continue my journey. I had a lot to learn and a place waiting for me where I could learn it.

That same evening I began my life in college. It was an uncomfortable transition to say the least. All of the other students seemed to have come from different worlds, and the little things I noticed had no effect on them. None of the other Bottom Line students were on campus yet, so I had to face this weirdness on my own.

I turned 18 at Smith, and it was a turning point for me. Within my first few weeks on campus, I received threatening IM messages from an anonymous student, full of racial slurs and threats to harm me. I was not afraid but had to report it because other students feared their safety. It was decided to move me out of the house and into a safety room on campus. It was Rochelle, a Bottom Line junior, who came to my aid and offered me a space to call home on campus to move past that situation. I quickly learned that even in a prestigious institution, you are never far from a learning experience.

Mapping Your Brain: The Neuroscience of Learning

Learning needs to be an act of joy, yet in schools these days, "education" has become a dirty word that kids reject when they step into the classroom. Joyful learning only happens when you are learning to use your own specific learning style in an active way. This is the neuroscience of learning that no one ever talks about.

Learning makes us human; it changes who we are and evolves what we can offer the world. Learning involves thinking and doing, action and reflection. Back in the old days, scientists believed that the human brain developed during childhood and that was it. Now we know the human brain changes all the time according to how and what we learn. It is a lifelong process.

The only constant in the world is change, and learning is the driver of change. As a successful human being, you need to be constantly learning to attract the kind of radical change that you need to succeed in your life. To understand how your brain learns, you need to take a closer look at neuroplasticity.

The brain adapts to the environment all the time, which means that your capacity to learn is never-ending. According to Dr. Judy

Willis,[21] neuroplasticity is the selective organizing of connections between neurons in your brain. That means that when you practice an activity or access a memory, your neural networks create electrochemical pathways and shape themselves according to that activity or memory.

When you stop practicing something, the brain eliminates or cuts back on the connecting cells. This gives you incredible insight into how to achieve your goals. It is basically saying that in order to be something, you need to practice it or immerse yourself in it in order for it to be true or materialize. Practice makes it permanent in other words.

Learning, therefore, is not some magical art that is only available to studious book nerds (hey, I was one!) in the classroom. It is available to everyone with a brain. All grey matter changes with experience, which means that you can train your way out of almost any situation. This single thought alone should be a motivator for you.

- Your brain is malleable, which means that practice is key. Repeating an activity, retrieving a memory, and reviewing material in a variety of ways helps build thicker, stronger connections in your brain.
- Learning is simply the practice of creating new or stronger neural connections. If you are bad at something, it is because your neural connection there is weak and needs to be strengthened. If you are good at something, it means that your brain has become hardwired to perform in that way.

Introduce joy[22] back into your learning process by playing to your strengths. Later in this section, you will find out which

21   Sara Bernard, Neuroplasticity: Learning Physically Changes the Brain, http://www.edutopia.org/neuroscience-brain-based-learning-neuroplasticity

22   Judy Willis, The Neuroscience of Joyful Education, http://www.ascd.org/publications/educational-leadership/summer07/vol64/num09/The-Neuroscience-of-Joyful-Education.aspx

learning style best suits you. Use it to become a knowledge sponge and to transform your life.

The Importance of Active Learning

Active learning can be defined as anything that involves a student doing things and thinking about the things they are doing. In other words, active learning deviates from the traditional classroom learning that only uses watching, listening, and taking notes to educate someone.

If neuroscience and neuroplasticity has proven anything, it is that learning is best optimized in practice. So while an artist can spend years learning theory, they will not be as talented as another artist that has spent the same amount of years physically painting. Practicing knowledge is almost as important as understanding it.

When you use active learning, it can reinforce material, concepts, and skills that you want to pick up quickly. Not only do you get real time feedback from practice but you can also streamline this practice according to your specific learning style. Passive learning is easy to ignore because it does not engage any of your senses.

Active learning,[23] on the other hand, makes sure that you are paying attention by filling your senses with everything you need to immerse yourself in the subject. Active learning is therefore experiential, mindful, and an engaging experience. When you mind is engaged, it is learning at a much greater rate because it is practicing knowledge. This in turn helps you forge those new neural connections and will make knowledge on the subject easier to access as your memories of the learning experience will be that much stronger.

I was very fortunate at school in that I was able to manage (more often than not anyways) the methods of learning that were

---

23 Active Learning, http://www.cte.cornell.edu/teaching-ideas/engaging-students/active-learning.html

proposed for everyone at the time. The truth is that many people simply cannot learn anything just by hearing it or passively taking notes off a blackboard. There are far better ways to learn, and you need to use them to improve yourself. Remember, learning and your education is your own responsibility and nobody else's!

Take a look at the difference between passive and active learning styles:

- Passive styles[24] include reading, listening, looking or seeing, and seeing/hearing. Lectures, presentations, demonstrations, and movies are all passive learning forms. You will know by now if you are able to learn using passive methods.

- Active styles include speaking and saying/doing, like giving a talk, group discussions, live practicing, dramatic presentations, tutoring, and simulations. In other words, that person that knows the material best is the teacher.

Use active learning styles to improve the way that you learn. Whether that means teaching someone else, practicing or demonstrating things to others, or simply getting more tactile in your approach to your education, all of these can help you retain more knowledge.

---

24 Active Learning, http://www.studygs.net/activelearn.htm

What are you actively learning in life right now? What should you be actively learning? Record them here:

_____

_____

_____

_____

_____

_____

_____

_____

_____

_____

Expanding Your Learning Experience

Education—or how we were made to think of it growing up—was something that happened when you got up in the morning for school. However, learning is far more important than that and deserves a much more prominent place in your life. After all, science has told us that it is what makes us able to do the things that we do.

Your own learning experience depends on how you think about "learning" in general. Every experience that you have in life is an opportunity to learn. Beyond this, you can actively pursue areas of interest so that your learning is focused and helps take you towards your goals. It is why artists revel in culture, history, and creativity—because these are catalysts.

I believe that you should shape your learning experience according to what you want to achieve in life and according to where your core interests lie. We are all attracted to certain areas of interest, and to be happy, it is important to explore these areas fully.

Beyond this, when you take the time to expand your learning experience, it facilitates a richer, deeper understanding of the subject that you are learning about. You will meet more people that enjoy what you enjoy, and your opportunities to indulge in discussion or reflection over key topics will improve.

There are several key areas that you consider when expanding your learning experiences. These can all help you gain fresh insight into the areas of interest you enjoy the most. Remember, these are lifelong learning opportunities, and throughout your life, you will add or remove elements to shape and focus where your knowledge centers lie.

- *Learning by doing*: Get out there and practice what you have just learnt. You will discover important knowledge that a book cannot tell you in the process.

- *Learning by talking*: Sit down with a group of people and discuss something to gain new perspectives and opinions on how things work.

- *Maintain the knowledge*[25] *that you have learned*: You cannot simply learn something and adopt a "set and forget" attitude in this day and age. Thanks to the Internet, what is known about your specific areas of interest is enough to keep you busy for the rest of your life and then some. Update what you know. and maintain your knowledge.

- *Growth learning*: This happens when you add skills to your skill range that you did not have before. Learning a new

25   Brian Tracy, Expand Your Mind: Importance of Lifelong Learning and Continuous Education, http://www.briantracy.com/blog/personal-success/expand-your-mind-importance-of-lifelong-learning-and-continuous-education/

language, for example, will make you a more valuable employee than before you knew that language. Skill knowledge improves your worth in job environments and will help you become successful in those roles.

• *Shock learning*: This type of learning happens when something contradicts or reverses a piece of knowledge or understanding that you took as the truth. Learning from failure and negative circumstances are instances of shock learning, and while they are never pleasant, there is always something to be gained from a bad situation.

How did you learn to be good at the last three things you learned? Record your process:

Learning in Context: New Horizons

At each stage of the education system, you are presented with a limited range of choices. These choices have been determined for you by other people, perhaps hundreds of years ago. The material you study in high school takes you to a college or university. The material you study at university helps take you into the world and, potentially, to success.

So it makes sense to understand the nature of learning. If you were bored at school, it may have been because the subjects did not interest you or because the teaching style was not a good match for your learning style. You might have enjoyed computers and art, for example, but were never specifically interested in either of them.

Learning in context[26] is a concept that has developed out of this conundrum. How does a car mechanic even know that they want to do that for the rest of their lives if there is no education guiding them in that direction at school? When you choose to learn in the context of your own interests throughout life—despite your age—things become easier.

Most people do not realize this naturally. They focus on school, and what they truly love and enjoy is outside the education system. This does not mean that what you love to learn about is unimportant. You have to place your learning experiences in a broader context then apply them to a scenario that leads to your success.

A car mechanic, for example, might decide to study mechanical engineering at a university. If they immerse themselves in the niche and learn as much as they can about this field in context—dedicating their time to it completely—the sky is the limit. This individual may invent a new kind of engine that replaces existing engines or own their own shop; with their foundation, the options are limitless.

---

26 Catherine A. Hansman, Context-Based Adult Learning, https://www.andrews.edu/sed/leadership_dept/documents/context_based_adult_.pdf

Do you learn in context? If so, name the five areas where you focus your learning most:

1. _____

_____

2. _____

_____

3. _____

_____

4. _____

_____

5. _____

_____

Learning is satisfying only when we get to share it with the world through application and acknowledgement. That means that we need to invest enough of our time into one specific learning branch to be able to contribute new and exciting things to that field.

How much time have you invested in "learning in context"? There is a big difference between thinking about learning more about something and actually doing it—actively, aggressively doing it. This is when the magic happens, and it is a step that few people make.

New horizons happen when you can wedge the door just wide enough to see the end goal. Then you can pursue it using the abundance of learning opportunities available to people today. Learn from others, study online, DIY study, or attend a college or university, but whatever you do, make sure that you center your learning around an area of interest that you love.

Have you ever heard of the concept of metacognition? This term stems from educational psychology, and while the term seems large, it is pretty easy to grasp. This concept allows students to be successful learners. Metacognition[27] means a higher order of thinking that involves a kind of active control over your cognitive processes during the act of learning.

A great example of metacognition happens when you stop halfway through an activity and evaluate your progress so that you can complete the task in a more efficient manner. It has been said that people that use metacognition more often are more intelligent. Put simply, metacognition is "thinking about thinking"—or noticing what one is thinking as they are experiencing it.

This conscious process allows for change, improvement, and enhancement of the learning process. You can learn to develop your metacognitive abilities at any time! To do this, you only need to focus on connecting new information to former knowledge, actively selecting thinking strategies that perhaps you have not tried before, or planning, monitoring, and evaluating the way that you think on an ongoing basis.

A person in charge of metacognition[28] is in charge of their behavior and, in my opinion, their destiny. A few simple strategies for doing this include the following:

- Identify and understand what you know and what you do not know.
- Talk about the things that you think, how it works, and what you can change.
- Assume responsibility for the way that you think, and regulate your thoughts.

27 Jennifer A. Livingston, Metacognition: An Overview, http://gse.buffalo.edu/fas/ shuell/cep564/metacog.htm

28 Elaine Blakey, Developing Metacognition, http://www.education.com/reference/ article/Ref_Dev_Metacognition/

- Evaluate how things could have been better with improved thoughts

The Lives I've Influenced (Interview Spotlight)

The relationships I have with people allow space to learn from and grow with each other. Here is what various people have learned, and the values that I try to extend to every new person that I meet.

Krystal Cummings: Iris has taught me that it's important to keep growing; you are in charge of your future.

Cynthia V. Gomez S: l learned a great deal from you as a mentor, a peer, and a sister. During my time at Smith College, I felt very alone and found in you someone I could trust and confide in. Being a Latina in a predominantly white institution was new to me, and I was unsure of how to handle myself in that environment. I had never been addressed as a "woman of color" nor did I find my color to be a distinguishing quality. As my first year came to an end, I joined the Latin@ organization on campus and began to identify myself proudly as a Latin@ Leader. In that time, I met many strong women, including yourself. I spent the rest of my college career learning from you. I learned how to be confident and to be a positive presence in the classroom. I learned where the best hiding places were in the library and around campus and that to persevere and make it in life, you need your network.

Leba: I learned patience, a commitment to friendship, personal strength, perseverance, and how to think big.

Michelle Restrepo: I don't think I'll ever forget the first time you ever kicked my butt with intense motivation when I needed it most. It was my senior year, finals time, and I was getting ready to pull yet another all-nighter. You saw me and simply said, "Get these finals done. Who needs sleep?!" You taught me how to prioritize, how to value myself, how to take control of my emotions. Most importantly, how to aim for happiness!

Stacy Diaz: I was in a very bad relationship for many years. It was unhealthy, I was unhappy, and goodness knows it affected me in every way. Through our friendship, I saw how happy I was just being me. I fostered a sense of independence, and although it took me a long time, I gained courage to get up and leave. You have always been independent, and I admired that. Through our experiences, you have taught me to value myself and put myself first because I deserve it.

Suly A.: You have taught me the beauty that hope brings into people's lives, especially when it comes at a time when they need it most. You inspire me to do the work I currently do now with "at-risk" youth. I see you, and many of us, in the lives of these teenagers. We need more stories like yours out there to serve as examples because our kids do not find that in the media; they don't have it in their circle of influence. They can only relate to the bad, the broken, and the ugly, and if a force that is stronger than them does not pull them out of that rut through motivation and the desire to live and to strive, a cycle is perpetuated—and the fact that this could have been you, but it is not, is a true blessing. You are an example of a very hard truth; what you go through has meaning, and the tough part is getting to the light at the end of the tunnel and turning your situation around because in your mind—failure DOES NOT EXIST. You have taught me that integrity is alive in friendship, which is something rare to find. You have taught me that the world is not a big enough place to hold you down, so why feel intimidated or overwhelmed.

**Where do you want to expand your learning?
Take a few moments to reflect:**

A Bullet Point Summary of Your Key Learning Areas:

CHAPTER 5

The Seven Key Styles of Learning

"There is no end to education. It is not that you read a book, pass an examination, and finish with education. The whole of life, from the moment you are born to the moment you die, is a process of learning."
Jiddu Krishnamurti

Learning is central to my existence. I thought I knew how important learning was in life, and then I went to Smith. In this world, everyone was on their A game all the time, and you had to keep up or get left behind. Being a top performer in my Boston public education still left gaps in comparison to peers at Smith, but there were no options to not make it work. I quickly discovered that learning was a much more complex animal than I had ever dreamed possible.

There are actually seven key learning styles that influence how you take in and remember information, and I believe that understanding how you learn on this micro level can help you become the studious human being you were always meant to be. I have realized that "smart" is relative, and it is more important to know how to make the most of your specific learning style.

Visual Spatial Learning Explained

To illustrate this point, I want to talk a little bit about my own style of learning. I am a visual spatial learner, which means that I think in pictures rather than in words. Due to this, I tend to learn holistically and can easily see the big picture in things, although it makes me less fixed on the smaller details.

I prefer using images, pictures, colors, and maps to organize information and communicate that information to others. My spatial sense is great, which gives me clear direction, and I can easily visualize things in my mind's eye. Dr. Linda Silverman tested gifted kids with this learning subtype and realized that they all shared specific traits.

For one, they primarily thought in pictures and were good at reading maps. They need to visualize words in order to spell them and were intuitive when solving problems. These kids were often late bloomers and had strong artistic, mechanic, or technological talents—and they tended to be highly focused on perfection.

I realized I was a visual-spatial learner[29] (even though I did not have a name for it) because of how I studied at school. I loved drawing out maps and used a whiteboard often. Even today, I use a whiteboard next to my desk at work each day to visualize almost everything. Answer these questions to find out if you are a visual-spatial learner:

- Are classroom environments not ideally suited to you so that your work at school perhaps does not reflect your actual intelligence?
- Do you have high grades in subjects that appeal to your visual learning style but are struggling to pass the other subjects that do not?

---

29 What Is a Visual Spatial Learner, http://www.time4learning.com/visual-spatial-learners.shtml

- Did school seem unnecessarily boring and repetitive? This may be because it is designed for auditory-sequential learners only.

To take advantage of your newfound visual-spatial learning skill, use visual aids when you learn. Buy a whiteboard, and grab a marker! You need to see or work with something to remember it and internalize the information. Study using creative methods to retain information; mind maps, word maps, video, and the Internet are excellent tools for you.

On a scale of 1–10, how much do you relate to visual spatial learning? Record your findings here:

Solitary Intrapersonal Learning Uncovered

The next kind of learning style is called solitary intrapersonal learning, and it means that you prefer to work alone and use self-study to gain understanding. People that enjoy this style of learning are private, introspective, and independent human beings.

They have excellent concentration skills and can easily focus their thoughts and feelings on a single topic for an extended amount of time. They are aware of their own thinking and can analyze different ways that they think or feel. Self-analysis is central to these individuals, and reflection on past events and accomplishments is common.

It is likely that you enjoy spending time alone and know yourself quite well. You have an independent mind and regularly seek to develop who you are. It may have even led you to purchasing this book so that you can gain a deeper understanding of yourself.

Your goals and objectives[30] in life have to be aligned with your personal beliefs and values, and you are nearly always personally interested in the topics that you enjoy studying. When you associate and visualize things, you concurrently think about how you would feel at the very same time, which can be an excellent tool for memory enhancement.

People that are solitary intrapersonal learners are driven by the way that they see themselves internally and who they could be in the future. Your thoughts also play a big role in your performance and personal safety. If you have to role-play, you do it with enthusiasm and creativity. Plus you love to use models that other people have built.

---

30   The Solitary (Intrapersonal) Learning Style, http://www.learning-styles-online.com/style/solitary-intrapersonal/

On a scale of 1–10, how much do you relate to visual spatial learning? Record your findings here:

_____

_____

_____

_____

_____

_____

_____

_____

_____

If you are a solitary intrapersonal learner like this, you are best suited to closed-door study on your own in a nice environment where you can focus and free your mind. Here are some questions that may help you identify yourself as this learning style:

- When you learn something, would you like some time to think about it afterwards?
- When you experience something new, do you think about how it made you feel?
- Do you often feel like exploring new things away from other people?
- Do you feel a need to retreat to research and develop your existing knowledge on a subject before speaking about it in public?

Self-study is like a super power. These students can learn on their own, and they can learn anything. It does not mean that they necessarily do well in school however, especially if the subjects do not entice them. Self-driven students need to experience a personal benefit when learning, so they are much more likely to daydream during boring lessons.

If you identify with these traits, then you would be best off learning by recording[31] personal thoughts and feelings in a blog or journal, setting goals, and having lots of alone time to reflect on your experience. Build portfolios, and immerse yourself in a subject to take advantage of your incredible focus.

Aural Learning Defined

One of the seven key learning styles is the aural or auditory-musical learner. This individual prefers using sound and music to learn new things and enjoy new experiences. If you use the aural style of learning, you will have a great sense of pitch and rhythm, and most often you will be able to sing, play an instrument, or identify the sounds of different instruments.

Music for you holds a special kind of magic, and it invokes strong emotions. You always notice the music playing in the background wherever you are—in an elevator, in movies, and in other media. You often hum or tap along to a song and regularly create your own little songs that you sing cheerfully without prompting.

Most often auditory learners[32] use sound, rhyme, and music to effectively learn new concepts. They also use sound recordings to provide an ambiance or background when they need to visualize something important during the learning process.

---

31   Dr. Mary Dowd, What Strategies Can I Use If I'm an Intrapersonal Learner?, http://everydaylife.globalpost.com/strategies-can-use-im-intrapersonal-learner-15805.html

32   The Aural (Auditory-Musical-Rhythmic) Learning Style, http://www.learning-styles-online.com/style/aural-auditory-musical/

When creating mnemonics or acrostics, you make the most of rhythm and rhyme and often set words to jingles or parts of a song. There is a good chance that you will have a specific song that makes you feel like you could take on the world. This song can anchor your emotional state and prime you for learning. Use it!

If you feel like you could be an aural learner, then perhaps you will recognize yourself in these questions. Aural learners tend to do better in school, which is an auditory environment.

- Does this ring a bell?
- Do you love setting words to rap or rhyming beats?
- Are you hyper aware when songs come on and are constantly listening to the music wherever you may be?

Your preference for learning[33] will be listening, discussing, talking, questioning, and recalling information because it all appeals to the auditory nature of your style. You naturally want to speak or hear the information to remember it. Audio books, movies, and other media are great learning tools along with anchoring your emotional state using music.

This is done by picking a specific song and then allowing your emotions to acclimatize to the message. Inspiring and motivating yourself to learn is easy because of this method. Aural learners like to talk in class and are better at listening than reading. They can recall lectures in great detail and struggle with reading-based learning.

To get the most out of your aural style of learning, speak up in discussion groups and seek out others that share your learning style. Listen to lectures, and record them to repeat the experience and maximize your memory retention. Getting someone to read out loud to you from a textbook is also helpful.

---

33 Auditory Learning: How to Use It to Help Learners Process Information, http://www.classroom-management-success.org/auditory-learning.html

On a scale of 1–10, how much do you relate to aural learning? Record your findings here:

_____

_____

_____

_____

_____

_____

_____

_____

Social Interpersonal Learning Exposed

The next kind of learning style belongs to the social interpersonal learner that loves to communicate with other people verbally and non-verbally. They usually have a strong sense of style, and people often go to them for advice. If you are sensitive to their motivations, feelings, or moods and you understand other people's perspectives well, then you may be this kind of learner.

Counseling others is also a draw for you, and you can enjoy learning in groups or in one-on-one scenarios with a teacher. When you bounce your thoughts off other people and hear their responses, it opens up your mind to new possibilities. You love group work and like it best when you click into a specific team—then magic happens.

As a social interpersonal learner, you learn through other people.[34] Social activities are high on your agenda, and you do not like doing "your own thing." You may be drawn to sports because team environments feel comfortable to you.

Your aim in a study environment is to work with others as much as possible because this is where you find your knowledge value. Role playing is a specific skill of yours and helps you in team and one-on-one environments. You need your associations and visualizations to work with other people so that they can be reflected back at you.

Practicing in groups and working through procedures helps you understand how to deal with a variety of situations. If this sounds like you, then there is a good chance that you are a social interpersonal learner. These questions can help you identify yourself:

- Do you want to work together on this? Tell me what you are thinking.
- Do you often need to run ideas by other people in order to formulate a complete picture of a situation?
- Do you learn by experiencing what other people have done incorrectly in group environments?

There are many learning strategies[35] that you could use to improve the way that you learn as a social interpersonal learner. Cooperative learning, giving and receiving feedback, and empathy practices are some great techniques along with group work, clubs, leadership development, and simulation situations.

Your learning style will work best when you are doing collaborative problem solving, coaching, and working in

---

34 Characteristics and Strategies for Different Learning Styles, http://www.csus.edu/indiv/p/pfeiferj/edte305/LearningStyle.html

35 The Social (Interpersonal) Learning Style, http://www.learning-styles-online.com/style/social-interpersonal/

community-related areas. Your social intelligence is very high, which means that you are very comfortable around other people and respect their boundaries. The best thing you can do for yourself is to organize regular study groups.

These groups can be made up of any number of different types of learner because you benefit from nearly all of them in a group environment. You will also be seen as a leader in these environments because of your social skills.

On a scale of 1–10, how much do you relate to verbal learning? Record your findings here:

Verbal Learning Explained

For verbal learners, you will find the written and spoken word the easiest methods of gaining knowledge. You find it easy to express yourself verbally and in writing because you probably have a real love for both. You are a natural at playing with the meaning or sound of words, and enjoy tongue twisters, rhymes, limericks, and poems.

You will also know the meaning of a lot of words and make a conscious attempt to expand your vocabulary when you come across words that you do not understand. You will regularly use these new words when talking to others. Verbal or linguistic learners prefer learning with words, both in speech and in writing.

Word-based techniques like assertions and scripting tend to be the most helpful with verbal learners. You can record your scripts using a tape recorder and review it later that way for maximum retention. This kind of learner finds that when they read content aloud, they want to make it dramatic and varied, like they hear it in their heads.

Role playing and working with others can also be beneficial as verbal exchanges help you find deeper meaning in knowledge. If you think and innovate linguistically[36] all the time, there is a good chance that you are a verbal learner. When at school, you enjoyed taking notes and communicating your ideas in writing.

Another factor is that verbal learners nearly always enjoy the "book" over the "movie" as linguistic information heightens the experience of a story. You are able to imagine it far better than anyone can visualize it in the real world. You should also find it easy to predict what is going to happen in a story next because you see patterns in the narrative.

To find out if you are a verbal learner or not, see if these questions pertain to you:

- The word you are looking for is? In other words?
- Do you have a vast book collection and spend a lot of time writing?
- Do you find joy in wordplay wherever it may be?

---

36 Overview of Learning Styles, http://artssciences.lamar.edu/_files/documents/nursing/orientation/overview_of_learning_styles.pdf

There are many strategies[37] that can help you maximize your learning style. While reading and writing are obvious methods, you can also use words, vocabulary activities, storytelling, tape recordings, typing, acting, humor, class discussions, and teaching to learn.

Research and playing with the sound of words can also be handy, along with interviews and literary analysis. If it involves language and words, it will reach you. Even better is if it involves language, words, and other people.

There is a good chance that you may be a verbal learner purely because you purchased this book. You might find real comfort in the knowledge that books provide and are therefore constantly seeking it out. This is an excellent method of ensuring long-term learning and continuous development.

On a scale of 1–10, how much do you relate to verbal learning? Record your findings here:

_____

_____

_____

_____

_____

_____

37   The Verbal (Linguistic) Learning Style, http://www.learning-styles-online.com/style/verbal-linguistic/

Physical and Logical Learning Defined

The final two learning styles are the physical or bodily-kinesthetic learning style and the logical or mathematical learning style. A bodily learner will prefer to use their body, hands, and sense of touch to retain knowledge, while the logical learner prefers using logic, reasoning, and systems to internalize knowledge.

The bodily learner[38] will focus on the sensations of the experience and will describe the physical feeling of their actions during assertions and scripting. They thrive when using physical objects in lessons and can be gifted writers or artists too. Role playing for these individuals to practice skills and behaviors is incredibly beneficial.

Your sense of touch teaches you about the world, and you enjoy thinking about things as you exercise. You notice and appreciate textures and are a "doer" more than a "thinker." Sitting and listening to a long lecture makes you bored out of your mind. You use large hand gestures and a lot of body language when you communicate.

To identify yourself as a physical learner, see if these questions appeal to you:

- Do you enjoy expressing yourself with your body?
- Are you more of a "hands on" kind of person, an "outdoors" kind of person?
- Do you love to dance, play sports, and create new movements in space?

A physical learner can learn via roleplaying, acting, dancing, miming, and drama. Other techniques might include demonstrations, workshops, simulations, field trips, and going on scavenger hunts. Inventing and being hands on with your work in a group environment is also very beneficial.

---

38   Barbara K Given, Chapter 5: The Physical Learning Style, http://www.ascd.org/publications/books/101075/chapters/The-Physical-Learning-System.aspx

A logical learner, however, uses their brain for logical and mathematical reasoning. They recognize patterns with ease and can see connections between meaningless content. You can work well with numbers, and math theory has never been a problem for you.

You like to work through problems in a systematic[39] way and create procedures to use in the future. You love numerical targets like budgets and agendas. You enjoy creating lists and adopt a scientific approach to explanations, often picking up on flaws in other people's logic, writing, or arguments.

To identify yourself as a logical learner, see if these questions appeal to you:

- Do you aim to understand the reasons behind every action or problem?
- Are you very set in your ways, and have you been described as stubborn?
- Do you love to play strategy games?

If you are a logical learner, your learning style can be enhanced by using computer games, building models, creating flow charts, outlining concerns, and indulging in the use of charts, graphs, diagrams, and maps. Number sequences are always fun, along with involving yourself in group study where you can express your love for these areas.

It is important to note that some people adopt multiple intelligences[40] and learning styles depending on how deeply they delve into the art and science of learning. Integrating different learning styles can be very useful for this individual, who has

---

39   The Logical (Mathematical) Learning Style, http://www.learning-styles-online.com/style/logical-mathematical/

40   Harvey Silver, Richard Strong, Matthew Perini, Integrating Learning Styles and Multiple Intelligences, http://www.ascd.org/publications/educational-leadership/sept97/vol55/num01/Integrating-Learning-Styles-and-Multiple-Intelligences.aspx

taught themselves how to learn using all of the styles available. This is controlled by their perception, which, as you know, can be expanded and developed through personal knowledge and self-development.

While you will you almost certainly favor one specific learning style, it is not uncommon to identify with or be able to learn effectively using other methods. Through mastery, interpersonal relations, understanding, self-expression, and kinesthetic knowledge, you can in fact teach yourself to learn efficiently using all of the aforementioned styles.

On a scale of 1–10, how much do you relate to physical and/or logical learning? Record your findings here:

Breakdown of Your Key Learning Styles:

_____

_____

_____

_____

_____

_____

_____

_____

_____

_____

Methods That Will Best Help You Learn:

_____

_____

_____

_____

_____

_____

CHAPTER 6

The Critical Art of Being Mentored

"The delicate balance of mentoring someone is not creating them in your own image, but giving them the opportunity to create themselves."
Steven Spielberg

Learning is not a solitary discipline. Even though you have discovered how your brain learns best, you still need guidance and instruction to optimize the process. There is no better way to do this than to find someone who knows more than you. I am a firm believer in mentoring and how rapidly it has a positive impact on the person being mentored.

When someone who has "been there, done that" gives you advice, it is often real, useful, and extremely valuable. Finding a mentor to help further your studies or improve your knowledge in a specific area is the most reliable method of getting up to speed on what you do not know. Mentoring is a critical art, and I would not be where I am today without it.

How to Find Your Ideal Mentor

After I received those threatening messages on campus, a Bottom Line student, who was also head resident, named Rochelle Valdez, took me under her wing during this fiasco.

I stayed with her as they found me a new house to stay in, and we bonded, coming from similar home backgrounds. As an undergrad at Smith, I had found a mentor in her. There are no fixed rules on who a mentor can be only that they have knowledge to impart. I was happy to have found someone who cared and was kind to me during a fairly rough time.

I enrolled as "undecided" but was interested in both engineering and psychology. I had an open curriculum and could mix my classes, which was great, but I knew that I would eventually have to commit to something. Engineering students, as I was told, rarely had time for anything but engineering—it was a very challenging thing to learn.

Inside, I rejected this argument and believed that I would be able to study engineering and pursue my other interests. Then the reality check happened! I had always fought hard to be as smart as I could be throughout school, but I quickly realized I was at a disadvantage in college. Many peers enjoyed access and resources to other types of learning in their upbringing that I had not even heard of as a young person.

I studied and read more, but my grades reflected the knowledge gap. Speaking frankly to my engineering advisor, I was told that I would be better suited to psychology, where it seemed to be easier for me—where I was getting A's—than engineering, where I was struggling just to get B's starting out. That conversation sank me as I felt I was being told this path was going to be too hard for me. I had to draw on internal strength to keep going.

Ultimately, even if things are hard as hell, no one can tell you what to do. If the fight is harder, fine. You have to do it! Some people mentor you well; others try to push you off your path. You need to recognize which is which and listen to your own instincts.

The Importance of Being Mentored Young

Mentoring is a way to guide someone towards a successful outcome based on the experience of someone who has already been through it. Back at Smith, I was a mentee and a mentor, and it had an enormous impact on my time there as a student.

Stripped down to its roots, mentoring[41] helps someone orientate and gives them someone that cares about their experience and trials during a challenging time. At school as well as in a working environment, being mentored by someone gives you the edge. Most students struggle along on their own without anyone to confide in or talk to.

Being mentored when you are young helps you avoid the traps that a lot of young people fall into, traps that may cause disaster and impact their future lives. Avoiding these traps is key to staying on track with your intended goals.

Being a mentee means more than simply avoiding common pitfalls and having a knowledgeable source of experience and advice on your side. In any environment, whether it is at school or at work, a mentor serves as an example and an endless inspiration to the people that they help. You are constantly reminded what you could achieve if only you try.

Proficiency, skill, learning quickly, and being responsible for the work that you put in are all areas that are greatly improved when you have a mentor. I like to think of mentors as "accelerators" because their first-hand experience is so useful it accelerates you through many obstacles that you otherwise would have struggled to overcome.

---

41   The Value of Mentoring, http://www.mentoring.org/about_mentor/value_of_mentoring

Can you identify any gaps in your knowledge a mentor might be able to fill? Record them here:

_____

_____

_____

_____

_____

_____

_____

_____

When you are mentored from a young age, you quickly grasp the importance of studying, working hard, and achieving your goals. Your mentor is there to teach you and to help you manage things that perhaps you have not been taught—like time management, scheduling, budgeting, and other areas where there may be gaps in your knowledge.

For many reasons, my mentors[42] quickly got me up to speed with things I did not even know I did not know and shared tips, tricks, and advice that helped me get ahead. I firmly believe that if they had not been there, I would have spent years trying to figure things out within myself instead of building based on others' knowledge.

---

42 Gregory P. Smith, The Importance of Having a Good Mentor, http://www. businessknowhow.com/manage/mentor2.htm

I saw such value in this process that I started focusing on a "mentoring" mind with many younger students at Smith. Whether it was facilitating a workshop to summarize campus resources to first years or leading a discussion on how to maneuver a job fair to problem solving a personal problem, sometimes just gaining awareness of options and having personal time with someone with more experience makes all of the difference. If you find yourself alone in unfamiliar surroundings and fighting for the success that you deserve, a mentor can be your biggest ally.

Plus, when you have a mentor in your corner, you know that you are not alone. There is someone that cares and someone who is watching out for you. This can be indispensable when you step into a new school or a new workplace where you are expected to thrive.

The Four Types of Mentoring

In my experience, there are four main types of mentor that you should seek out when you have arrived in a new location in your life. Fast orientation can be an advantage over other students or employees who are starting out alongside you. Look for these four main kinds of mentoring[43] in your mentor, and you will be off to a great start.

Type 1: Role Modeling

The first type of mentoring happens when a mentor's attitudes, values, and behaviors are the basis for your own. You will emulate the mentor in these areas and model their behavior. As a result, you will get further ahead with your goals.

The mentor will teach using dialogue and troubleshooting and by overcoming obstacles as the mentee learns approaches, attitudes, and values that help in this new environment.

---

43   Types of Mentoring Functions, http://www.educause.edu/careers/special-topic-programs/mentoring/about-mentoring/types-mentoring-functions

Type 2: Acceptance / Confirmation Mentoring

When both the mentor and the mentee derive a sense of self from positive regard conveyed by the other, that is when confirmation mentoring happens. This is an emotionally supportive type of mentoring that is extremely useful for people that need support and encouragement.

The student, for example, is given support when they need it, and a bond of trust is formed between the two people. There is a foundation of acceptance, risk-taking is encouraged, and experimentation and innovation are encouraged to uncover hidden potential.

Type 3: Counseling

Counseling is the purest form of mentoring, and it enables the individual to explore personal concerns that might interfere with a positive sense of self and career accomplishment. The mentor counsels the mentee through emotional, social, and intellectual challenges.

As a result, the mentee gets comfort in discovering that doubts and concerns are shared in a confidential environment, where there is always help waiting for them.

I was very lucky to have my mother's best friends, my sister's godparents, act as a second set of parents while I was growing up. Egle and Johnny were amazing counselors to me as a young child. I remember countless times on our Pennsylvania family trips, where my sister and I would sleep, and how it felt like such a safe space for me. I could always open up and talk about my personal issues at home and know I had a sounding board to help me work through my struggles.

Type 4: Friendship

At its heart, this type of mentoring evolves into friendship as social interaction results in mutual liking and understanding.

Enjoyable informal exchanges about work and non-work experiences become the basis for a good relationship that transcends the definition.

There is probably no better example in my life for this than my Tío Pito. My Tío was incarcerated at a young age and was held in the prison system for most of my life. He started writing me letters and drawings when I was a child to build a communication channel. I was able to get really consistent with him in college, and he was my biggest supporter. When I felt like I had no family support in college, he was always there for me without hesitations. He was there for me when I was getting kicked out of my mother's home and when I was scared about everything that I was learning about myself and seeking self-acceptance. He would share with me about his work, his studies, and the inner emotions he was reconciling with as well. I saw a lot of myself in him, and through the years, we have learned so much from each other. I catch myself with the biggest grin now that is he just a text message away from me.

The mentee will feel like a peer or a colleague and not just a student or someone that needs to be taught. This is extremely useful when you step into a new environment and need friends to introduce you to other like-minded people.

Ideally, you want to find a mentor that utilizes all four types of mentoring so that you can get the most out of your interactions with them. A great mentor will be a cheerleader, a challenger, an educator, and a connector. They will support you, force you to greater heights, teach you, and help you find your way to new social groups and experiences.

Developing Your Mentor Partnership

Make no mistake, a mentor relationship is first and foremost a partnership.[44] Both of you have to be on board in order for it to work well. If the mentor does not truly want to help, you will not gain any of the benefits of being mentored. At the same time, if you are not willing to be mentored, you will not take any advice or seize on any opportunities offered.

Like any real relationship, mentorship is a two-way street. To develop a mentor partnership that will provide you with everything that you need, follow this simple process:

Step 1: Ask yourself why you need a mentor: Determine why you need a mentor to establish reasons for initiating the relationship. Your needs are important, and you have to be able to communicate them to find a mentor that will fit in with them. Do a thorough inventory of your values and emotional needs too because they matter; then detail why you actually need a mentor for the sake of clarity.

Step 2: Choose your ideal mentor: You will have to build a goal list for any new mentoring partnership so that you can ensure that your needs are met. Write down all the qualities that you want your ideal mentor to possess along with personal, professional, and social traits. Find someone to admire that you could easily emulate. Make sure that your worldviews are aligned.

Step 3: Recruit your mentor: The next step is to take your list of goals and objectives and actually find a match. I have found that I have never built a successful mentoring relationship by outright asking. I have found through the years that mentoring candidates may feel overwhelmed by a heavy weight or burden associated with the responsibility of being a "good" mentor or, worse, provide forced answers to you or create an invisible wall

---

44   The Eight Steps to Developing Successful Mentoring Partnerships, http://www. jodidavis.com/pdfs/8stepsmentoring.pdf

that you will never be able to get through. The best relationships have always been created organically; that is, I started by creating a request to share an experience together (go out for coffee, have a discussion on a shared topic, go for a hike) and then used that time to make the most of it. Ask questions that challenge the candidate to think, and give guidance without knowing. If you are successful, you will know because chances are these "forums" will continue to happen. Before long, you have built an organic mentoring relationship.

Step 4: Set the boundaries of your relationship: A mentor partnership[45] needs to be confidential, where honest communication and trust are nurtured carefully and consistently. Be clear with your desires and expectations, and express how you will honor your mentor's wishes. Allow room for flexibility, and remember you are looking to create a long-term relationship and not one that will last for a few months. Clear, transparent communication will happen naturally as long as you have step three down!

Step 5: Understand your roles: In most cases, clearly defined roles in a partnership are critical. The mentee takes responsibility to manage the relationship—from how often you get together to topics and conversation. You are in the driver's seat. A great mentee is proactive, prepared, and organized for when they have an outing with a mentor.

Step 6: Set goals: Early in your partnership it is a good idea to formalize your objectives and prioritize specific goals (even if just for yourself). Consider how you will approach things and whether the process will be formal or informal. Remember to be flexible with your mentor and make it sustainable for the long haul.

Step 7: Evaluate your progress: A good mentoring partnership is consistently evaluated. Goals need to be achieved and progress made by the mentee. Candid feedback is therefore a vital element

---

45   Training Introduction, http://www.pcaddick.com/

of building a great partnership. Have 3-, 6-, and 12-month reviews planned.

Step 8: Finalize your partnership: A mentoring partnership done well is emotional, so it is important that whenever you close the relationship, express thanks and appreciation. Give them honest feedback so that they can improve as a mentor, and discuss staying in touch.

Describe your ideal mentor partnership here:

What to Expect out of Mentorship

Different mentors have different sets of rules, but as long as they are adhering to the four types of mentoring, you should be able to get the most out of the partnership. One of the most challenging elements of any mentoring partnership is setting expectations. Without clearly defined expectations, the relationship can run into a number of common problems.

In my experience, some of these can include the mentor not spending enough time with the mentee, the mentee not sharing their real problems or emotions with the mentor, and one side of the partnership feeling as though the other is not fully "in it," which results in a breakdown of trust, whereby the benefits of the partnership are lost.

Mentors[46] do not exist to do your work for you, but they can often become involved in helping you achieve specific work goals or grades, if that is what you want. Every relationship will come with a unique set of expectations according to your goals. The key here is to strike a balance so that the two of you are communicating well, sharing, and forging ahead.

A good mentor will support your work and life balance goals while helping you build an ever-expanding network of people that can help you achieve these goals. They will enhance your personal leadership skills, will improve your interpersonal skills, and will facilitate better communication in your relationships.

Mentors that do great work also help you develop new perspectives and expanding possibilities, and they teach you vital problem-resolution skills. Most of all, they are experts on where you are and can help you navigate the culture of your environment so that you can gain maximum benefit from it. This helps you plan for better things in the future.

Expect your mentor[47] to help you set and achieve goals. You will not do all of the talking as this is a partnership after all—which implies knowledge sharing. Your mentor will communicate concepts, ideas, and rules to you, and you will respond. The two-way dialog will help you gain clarity and will keep you in line.

---

46   Annie Pilon, What to Expect and Not to Expect From a Business Mentor, http://smallbiztrends.com/2014/02/what-to-expect-from-a-business-mentor.html

47   Dr. Rodney Cate, What Does Good Mentoring Look Like?, https://www.ncfr.org/professional-resources/career-resources/students/what-does-good-mentoring-look

Organization and preparation is important when seeing your mentor, as their time is limited and they could be mentoring other people or putting time into other domains of their life. It is therefore your responsibility to orientate them when you see them and update them on your progress. Each meeting should be viewed as an opportunity, even if you become close friends with your mentor.

Mentorship can be the best thing you ever got involved in if you choose the right mentor and make sure that your relationship remains important and balanced. Expect good communication from your mentor as a bare minimum as they will need this to get through to you. Honest feedback and introductions to new groups of people can also be expected.

Remember that you do not need to limit yourself to one mentor. I have mentors in all areas of life in which I am actively building on from business building, engineering, writing, music, etc. Your main goal is to find those people that will help you get to where you want to be and do your part to maintain the partnership for as long as it makes sense to the both of you.

What do you expect from someone who is mentoring you? Record it here:

Accelerated Learning: The Experience

Have you ever heard the saying "the wise learn from the experience of others"? It is an old Romanian proverb, and it still rings true to this day. Mentoring partnerships are one of the fastest, easiest ways to transfer important knowledge between people to ensure success. I saw the process in action from Bottom Line on, and it really does work.

If you are a believer in continual learning, then you know that you can never reach the point where you know enough to settle. The entire goal with learning in any new environment is to get up to speed as soon as possible so that you can learn how to "dial in" to the system and take advantage of any and all opportunities that lie within it.

You will find this at college and at any new workplace. There are always systems, processes, and skills that you will need in a new environment, and nothing gets them to you faster or more efficiently than mentoring. Think of all the key learning types we spoke about earlier. Nearly all of them benefit from one-on-one interaction.

I like to call the process of being mentored "accelerated learning" because that is what it does in the end. Not only does it educate you quicker but it also gives you pieces of knowledge that you just cannot find anywhere else, especially not in books or online. People and their experience with a place in real time are valuable knowledge sources.

There is a never ending supply of knowledge to learn through someone else's eyes. During your career at college, you may have one mentor or five. The experience is really up to you! Learning can be accelerated at your own pace or at a blinding pace. Everything is always on a timer, so I strongly urge you to "accelerate" as much as possible.

Working hard, smart, and consistently is all it takes to impress even the most insistent mentor. You become a reflection of their mentoring skills, so they will want you to succeed. It is completely up to you to listen and take advantage of every little piece of advice that comes your way. Getting into this habit is a lifelong skill!

When you experience good mentoring, you will not be able to live without it again. I personally find great value in always having at least a few mentors in my corner. I have coined them as my personal board of directors who are experts and guides in domains of my life in which I am building on. I believe it has helped accelerate my learning to a point where I have become an incredibly valuable knowledge resource for others so that I can pay it forward, which generates even better opportunities.

Accelerated learning[48] is a rollercoaster experience, but if you dare to take it, this can be the ride of your life. Few people are bothering with mentorship programs because they do not see the value in them or feel like it takes up too much time and effort. People that have relied on few resources at some point in their life know better. We understand that people can have major influence on your life and know how to make the most of our resources. Align with the right mentors, and you will take off!

---

48   Jerry Jao, Why CEOs Need Mentors – They Accelerate Learning, http://www.
entrepreneur.com/article/239682

Identify your core reasons for needing a mentor:

Prioritize your reasons for needing a mentor:

DRIVE: CAN YOU SHAPE WHO YOU ARE?

CHAPTER 7

Discovering Your True Purpose

"Success is almost totally dependent upon drive and persistence. The extra energy required to make another effort or try another approach is the secret of winning."

Denis Waitley

The next element in the WEDGE Effect equation is drive. Once you have settled on your wish and have closed that knowledge gap—or perhaps begun to close that gap—you will need to have the drive to see it through. You have the power to shape who you are now and who you will become. But you will never get there without motivation, determination, and focus.

There are many things in life that drive us. Our true purpose is the most authentic driver of all as it draws us closer towards our most desperate desires of the heart. When you spend your time on your true purpose, it makes you happy. When you are happy, you can learn, grow, and achieve real success in your endeavors. That is how this whole thing works!

My Engineering Education

I spent a lot of time thinking about that engineering advisor and what she had said to be about my major. That is the thing with advisors, counselors, and teachers—sometimes they do not see the best in their students. Sometimes they try to help by making things easier, and they discount whether or not you are willing to fight for what you want.

I had come from a different, rougher childhood than most, and so I decided to think for myself and ignore the advice she gave me. I continued to take courses in engineering, psychology, and African-American studies. I did not stick to the conventional coupling of courses as I was told to do; instead, I pursued my own interests.

During the summer after my first year, I was on my way to work at my engineering internship when I was rear-ended on the highway with a car driving so quickly that I ended up in the middle of a four-car accident. I was left with torn muscles from my neck down to my legs. It required physical therapy five times a week for the rest of the summer and shorter hours during my internship because I could not sit for long durations as well as a few trips to the hospital to receive back injections to reduce the pain. Even when it was time to start my sophomore year, I was dealing with loads of physical pain, and I could have taken a break, but I knew I needed to keep going.

There were times when I was working four jobs on and off campus (to help with my loans, my books, and to enjoy college every once in a while), taking 20 credits, doing three labs, and participating in several student organizations all at once—while mentoring up-and-coming students. I knew that in the beginning I would need to adjust, but I also knew that it would not take me long. I understood my potential, and I wanted to make good use of it.

My final two years at Smith were the best yet. I achieved 4.0 semesters and landed on the Dean's list in my junior and senior years. There was one engineering professor who kept me fascinated in the classroom as she broke away from conventional engineering education and forged her own path forward.

Social justice and global awareness were woven into her narrative, which forced us all to think more holistically about things. I naturally gravitated in her direction, and we built an amazing relationship as I worked with her. She was one of the most incredible mentors that I ever had, and I was very pleased to have found her.

She reinforced once again that you forge your own path. Everything is your choice, and you can do things your own way. Demolishing obstacles is possible in any circumstance. Shaping who you are is a personal responsibility of the highest order.

What Purpose Means in Life

If you do not know where you are going, you will never get there. Sometimes translating the innermost desires of our hearts means putting our life purpose into words. Everything you do in life leads you down a specific path. Every choice that you make results in something—whether that something is positive or negative.

Purpose is the thing that gives it all meaning. I believe that everyone has a purpose and that it only needs to be discovered. When I was in school, my sole purpose was to work hard and open doors to new opportunities that I would otherwise not have exposure to. I wanted it so badly that nothing could stop me. But this was not my life purpose; that is a far more complex concept.

However, like the goals[49] that drove me to work hard and produce extraordinary results in school, your real life purpose also drives you to do things. It can take you towards specific careers and sets a whole range of goals for you that will take a lifetime to

---

49   Finding Meaning and Purpose in Your Life, http://www.oprah.com/spirit/
Finding-Meaning-and-Purpose-in-Your-Life

achieve. Finding your life purpose will give meaning and weight to every decision that you make.

If you do not have this purpose behind you, you will feel aimless and wandering. Nothing you do will fill that need inside you, and this is the thing that ultimately makes us all happy. When you have a clear purpose—even if it is a short-term one—it will make a world of difference.

Being unmotivated, full of doubt and insecurity, and directionless are all consequences of not having a purpose. Your life purpose is to find out what gets you up in the morning—the calling that makes you who you are.

In life, purpose is the ingredient that nurtures motivation, drive, and energy. If you do not have it, you will never be able to stick to anything. People say that they "procrastinate" about things, which is why they cannot succeed. However, this is not telling the full truth. Procrastination is simply a byproduct of not having a strong enough purpose.

Purpose is fueled by genuine passion[50] and practice; the more you work towards it, the better you feel, and the more you want to work towards it. That is how it works. If you are unable to get something done, it is because you have been approaching it for the wrong reasons. You need to find your authentic purpose first then use it to drive your goals.

Baking might be something that you love, but you never get around to doing it because you lack purpose. If you look deep within and realize that you can bake cakes for a homeless shelter, this gives you a purpose. It is in alignment with your personal purpose of serving those in need. Suddenly you have good reasons to do what you love. It is a simple formula but one that people cannot see in their own lives.

Purpose is the driving force, and it is about time you discovered yours.

---

50   Leo Babauta, How to Find Your Life Purpose: An Unconventional Approach, http://zenhabits.net/life-purpose/

Can you identify five core passions that may point to your life purpose? Record them here:

1. _____

_____

2. _____

_____

3. _____

_____

4. _____

_____

5. _____

_____

The Weird Questions That Work

Finding out what your purpose is in life is one of the most difficult tasks a person has to work through. For me, I knew that I wanted to help people, but I also had so many other interests I had no idea where I would end up. Some people know where their purpose[51] lies from a young age; others are still looking for it at age 70.

There are some weird questions that I have come across in my day that can help you uncover your life purpose. Work through these questions, and you will see how something in particular comes to light. Then use this purpose to navigate through your life decisions.

---

51 Mary Jaksch, 15 Questions That Reveal Your Ultimate Purpose in Life, http://goodlifezen.com/15-questions-that-reveal-your-ultimate-purpose-in-life/

1. **On the worst day in the world, what can you still see yourself doing?**

   The truth is that even the best things in the world suck sometimes. While I love helping others, I still have bad days! If you can see yourself doing something specific on the worst day ever, then you clearly have a passion for it. Use this as a guiding tool.

2. **Which activity do you love so much it keeps you from eating and sleeping?**

   We all have activities in our lives that we enjoy so much that we lose track of time. These are areas where we should be investing most of our time. If it keeps you from eating and sleeping, then it must be something that means a lot to you.

3. **What would be the most embarrassing thing that could happen to you in your career?**

   Think of the work that you have done in the past. Often what we care about most is where we are most vulnerable. People will do anything to prevent themselves from feeling embarrassed about something they care about, and so they avoid it. This may be the area that you are hiding because it is so important to you.

4. **You are a super hero, but you have no powers. It is up to you to save the world, one person at a time. How do you do it?**

   Everyone is given specific gifts and talents that they can use to do good things and help others in the world. What are your super powers? Knowing how you can use these to make the world a better place is a step towards defining your true purpose.

> **If you had to choose one thing to do for the rest of your life, what would it be?**
>
> _____
>
> _____
>
> _____
>
> _____
>
> _____
>
> _____

Forget What Everyone Else Says

Some people have a way of getting into your head about who you really are. Parents project their expectations on you and try to steer you in specific directions. You might feel like you are an artist for example, but because your father knows artists do not make much money, he will encourage you to go to school to become a lawyer.

Everyone in the world will have their opinion about who you are and what you should be doing with your life. Ultimately it is a decision that comes from within yourself. And it does not have to be a static one. Your purpose in life can change, or you can find that you have several life purposes that are all related to a similar field.

The moment you internalize what other people want from you—or what they say you are—you will be unhappy. It makes more sense to answer this very important question alone. After all, no one knows you better than you know yourself. You are a unique blend of skills, talents, opinions, and emotions.

I have seen many great people being thrown off their life path[52] in order to please others. I have seen this both in personal and professional contexts. When you start taking other people's opinions into account, you may become diverted or preoccupied or stray off your personal path. This is when your true purpose becomes diluted and you stop being fulfilled and happy.

Using the artist analogy again, you may know that you are an artist but only care about sculpting. Your family keeps telling you what an amazing painter you are, and your paintings sell well, so you keep doing them. You know you love sculpting and that painting does not bring the same joy. It seems like everything you do is trying to get you back to the point where you can sculpt, but others' opinions and influence on you keeps you away.

People are always full of opinions, but look around—are they a product of the perspective they are giving you? Are they aware of and living their purpose? This is not an easy journey, but nothing worth doing is ever easy. You must learn to tune yourself to listen and take in criticism and words that can knock you off your life path, diminish your time investment in your ultimate purpose, and determine when you need to follow your own gut against it.

You cannot always "do the right thing" if the right thing does not align[53] with who you are or what you need from life. Following set rules or doing what society expects from you is a great way to end up completely unhappy. I cannot imagine how unhappy I would have been if I had dropped out of engineering and not followed my gut to the path I wanted to create.

It is good to play to your strengths, but better to know that anything can be a strength if it is practiced often enough. Never

---

52 Joshua Becker, 10 Unconventional Habits to Live Distraction-Less, http://www. becomingminimalist.com/distraction-less/

53 James McWhinney, 6 Powerful Questions That Will Change Your Life Forever, http://tinybuddha.com/blog/6-powerful-questions-that-will-change-your-life-forever/

forget that! Take everyone else's opinions and rules with a pinch of salt. At the end of it all, you want to live your own life and forge your own path. It has nothing to do with what anyone else wants from you.

Name three things you do today that you do not enjoy doing but do because someone else expects it from you:

1. _____

_____

2. _____

_____

3. _____

_____

Shaping Your Personality: Process of Elimination

There is only one core technique that I know of that helps you find out who you are. This technique is not hard—it is very easy—yet few people do it. When I speak about shaping your personality, I am talking about directing your energy to find out who you really are and what you really want from life.

Some people believe that our personalities are formed based on our environment, our parents, and the experiences that we have faced growing up. While this may be true for your foundation, it is also true that your personality never stops evolving. It makes sense, then, to get out into the world and experience new things. The more you experience, the more you will understand.

The only technique that works when trying to find out who you are is to get out there and live life. You cannot find out what you like and dislike using the process of elimination if you are shut away at home or confined to "safety zones." A comfort zone exists because it is comfortable, but great people do not live there. They push boundaries and break rules.

The easiest way to shape your personality[54] is therefore to be exposed to as much "life" as the world has to offer. Go to new places and meet new people—experience something new! Test boundaries, and challenge what makes you comfortable. Believe me, the world has enough "new" to last your entire lifetime. That is why well-travelled people seem so jovial; they have seen a lot of life.

The more information you can collect about your likes and dislikes, the more knowledge you will gain about yourself. All of this forms the unique picture that is you. It is true that you can shape your personality in different directions according to your life goals. If your purpose is to be a business leader, then you need to build your skillset appropriately for that kind of role.

Even if you have been a shy person all of your life, with six months' worth of training, you can turn this notion of yourself on its head. It is a matter of setting goals that will lead you down the right paths so that you can achieve success.

Personality[55] is simply how you think, feel, and behave in this life. Thoughts, feelings, and behaviors can all be influenced and changed. You can accomplish these goals by improving your drive by first setting a life purpose for yourself and then working to repair the parts of your personality that do not fit in with these goals.

---

54 10 Ways to Improve Your Personality, http://www.essentiallifeskills.net/improveyourpersonality.html

55 Michael W. Kraus, The Power to Be Me, https://www.psychologytoday.com/blog/under-the-influence/201201/the-power-be-me

Start with who you do not want to be, and work from there. It is much easier to say "no, I do not like this" than "yes, I love this," so the process of elimination can get you off to a good start. This is the same with experiences; try it once, and if you do not enjoy it—at least you gave it a shot. Anything is possible once your life purpose is set. You only need to put in the time and the work and have the drive to get it all done.

Name five personality traits you have a hard time working with: Record them here:

1. _____

_____

2. _____

_____

3. _____

_____

4. _____

_____

5. _____

_____

THE WEDGE EFFECT

The Lives I've Influenced (Interview Spotlight)

Your life changes as you grow up. To illustrate this point, I asked several people about my childhood who I was then and who I became once I had realized my life purpose.

Amanda N. Coats: In your late teen/earlier twenties, you were a different person than I know now. You have truly become the woman I knew was somewhere inside you. You have always been intelligent, and that has not changed. However, the angry person that I felt you were holding onto has pretty much diminished as far as I can tell. You have evolved into this beautiful person who can take it and dish it out without the harshness and/or lack of feeling I felt you had before. You are strong, but that "tough" exterior that you showed so many is now more of a welcoming confidence that evokes authority but ease at the same time. And you're healthier now, which I am very proud of you for doing!

Evelyn Marie González: Childhood had its good and bad moments. From the outside, our life was seen as great and easy, but on the inside, it was very different. It was challenging, and the environment was not conducive to success in many ways. It was very cutthroat and hard many times, and it was hard to understand why things were the way they were, especially as a child. Life was confusing, and it was hard to deal with so much instability. We were responsible for getting good grades and getting our chores done at home, and high expectations were set, although we weren't always given the tools to set us up for success.

Cynthia V. Gomez S.: I can describe difficult times with your father. You have always proven to be very strong, even to the point of seeming defiant—a trait that is unappealing for a woman to possess in our culture. One of your responsibilities has been to care for your siblings while caring for yourself.

Leba: I would describe your teen years as different, quick tempered, but always inclusive to others around you. Off center

118

in character and somewhat emotionally one ended. (If anger or irritation got control, it would consume your emotional spectrum.)

Stacy Diaz: I met you when you were in the tail end of your high school years. I remember you telling me that you were looking for scholarships and colleges and you used to share them with your friends. On one occasion, a friend ended up getting a scholarship you both applied for, and you were genuinely happy for her. I think that those types of memories remind me of why we became friends and why you are the way you are. Regardless of the life circumstances that were passed down, you were always about helping others. You also advocated for yourself. Seeing you move up and bloom throughout those young adolescent years was a blessing. My Smith experience wouldn't have been the same without you. You did have a lot in your heart, deeper than many

Where do you believe your true life purpose lies?

Tier your life goals by order of importance:

_____

_____

_____

_____

_____

_____

_____

_____

_____

CHAPTER 8

How to Inspire Yourself to Greatness

"As you navigate through the rest of your life, be open to collaboration. Other people and other people's ideas are often better than your own. Find a group of people who challenge and inspire you, spend a lot of time with them, and it will change your life."
Amy Poehler

could understand. You would often mask your pain with being "loud" and "funny," but once I got to understand your upbringing on a deeper level, it made our connection easier, and I was able to see through the façade. This happened when you were still a teen—around 18. Once you began to open up to those that truly cared (and care) about you, you began to feel more comfortable in your skin.

reatness is something that most people want, but after a
few feeble, failed attempts, they convince themselves that
"greatness" is impossible. I believe that there is greatness inside
everyone, but the dysfunction lies with how we see ourselves and
what we know about the science of inspiration.

Being "inspired" is something that had been assigned to
artists, writers, and genius minds like Albert Einstein, Steve Jobs,
or Picasso, but it is actually quite a common process. When you
know how it works and why, you can harness this process to kick
yourself into gear and become the great person that you were
always meant to be.

Your Ideal Blueprint: Knowing the Truth

Inspiration[56] sounds like a "grand" idea. In a sudden fit of
inspiration, an artist will paint something masterful. But no one
knows where inspiration comes from. It might be hard for us to
know how or where it even pops up.

Inspiration focuses on those "epiphany" moments that shed
light on a problem that you have been working on. If you have
been waiting to feel inspired to work, you have been doing it all
wrong. Inspiration does not work that way. In fact, inspiration is
an active process, not a passive one. The more you work and dwell
on a problem, the greater your chances become.

Your ideal method of becoming inspired[57] will be different
from mine. Some people get inspired because of certain types
of music, literature, or friends. The thing is, inspiration is not
just something you can turn on like a light switch, so why do you
try? Waiting for inspiration to strike to get something done is like

---

56   Eric Ravenscraft, The Science of Inspiration (and How to Make It Work for
You), http://lifehacker.com/the-science-of-inspiration-and-how-to-make-it-work-
for-1467413542

57   Cindi May, The Inspiration Paradox: Your Best Creative Time Is Not When You
Think http://www.scientificamerican.com/article/your-best-creative-time-not-when-
you-think/

waiting for a pen to write of its own accord.

Do not mistake inspiration for perspiration! Hard work is not the same as having an "Aha!" moment. People try to excuse hard work away all the time by saying that they are not "inspired" to work. But the greatest people of the last 100 years were not perpetually inspired. The common feature that they shared was that they were all incredibly hard workers.

> **What do you work hard at in your life and why? Record them here:**
>
> _____
>
> _____
>
> _____
>
> _____
>
> _____

Productivity is the key—and the answer to the endless inspiration question. To become inspired, first of all you have to make it happen. You have to physically engage in something that you find inspiring. Even then, you might only get "prepared" for the work to come. Most days this preparation will be enough to take you through your workload.

Then, on the odd occasion, you will feel truly inspired, and you will have great ideas. The ideas come from randomized moments of insight, not hard work, and the work will never get done by inspiration alone. Sorry, but if you are going to be great, you have work to do.

Name five things that motivate you to work: Record them here:

1. _____

_____

2. _____

_____

3. _____

_____

4. _____

_____

5. _____

_____

How Motivation Works and Where to Get It

Inspiration and hard work are two common elements that are preceded by one single thing—motivation. Most people confuse motivation for inspiration because they do not want to take responsibility for the fact that they do not feel like working or cannot motivate themselves to put in the extra effort. "Extra effort" is a superpower in itself.

Motivation is a practice, not a passive "feeling" that strikes. Like anything else, it takes hard work to stay motivated and strong levels of self-discipline to hold it all together. Every goal in life needs to be matched with a plan or a strategy that will help it come to fruition. Once you have a strategy and a goal, motivation becomes something that you can map.

With your ultimate purpose as the driver, motivation[58] is a short-term concern, but it is only half of the concept. The full word is actually "self-motivation" because that is where real motivation comes from—inside yourself. Other people can prompt you to work or remind you to get started, but only you can decide what to do, when, and how well.

That is why motivation is a tricky one. It plays with our moods and emotions and becomes wrapped up in our current mental state. The world is a busy place, and with less and less focus around, people that can self-motivate are getting even rarer than before. The average person would rather do the bare minimum than get up and do something.

Would you like to learn how to achieve any goal? The secret is motivation. This is the second driver behind your ultimate purpose that gets things done in the short term. Whether you need to wake up early, exercise, or get that paper written, motivation can be your best friend in life. It will help you towards success faster than inspiration ever would.

This is due to one simple idea—goal stickiness. If you can stick to a plan and complete it from start to finish, you win. Every time. Too many people cannot do this. They cannot sit down and force themselves to execute the plans they put in place. They jump from one idea to the next, giving up each time because things are "too hard."

I learned that when people say things are "too hard," what they really mean is that there is too much hard work to do, and the success did not come quickly enough. Motivation, by its very nature, keeps you going when you do not want to go. It is natural for you to not want to work that hard, but with the right reasons, you commit and do it anyway.

That is why the best motivation for anything comes from you.

---

58 The Ultimate Guide to Motivation – How to Achieve Any Goal, http://zenhabits.net/the-ultimate-guide-to-motivation-how-to-achieve-any-goal/

You have to want the end result long enough to sit through the trials and hard work. You need to nurture a passion for the "next step" in your plans. I am going to show you many ways to do this so that you become a motivation pro like me.

The Science of Self-Motivation

To succeed in anything in life, you need a healthy dose of self-motivation on demand. Some people are better at it than others because it requires a certain level of commitment, discipline, and willpower to get right. Motivation is where that magic begins. It allows you to get through an entire book in a few hours.

It allows you to complete that essay in one day even though it took you six consecutive hours. When you are not afraid of self-motivation, the world is at your feet. Once you have a plan in place (and you always need a plan to become motivated), you must act with speed and a positive attitude and be efficient at what you do.

That means cutting out distractions and keeping your mind focused on the task at hand. With the Internet and other daily distractions around today, this is not easy, but it can be done. Time management and energy allocation are also two important ingredients in your motivation soufflé. There is a real science behind staying motivated for a long time.

- You need to be completely committed. There is a job to do, and you will get it done no matter what happens. Through drama, illness, and lack of sleep, no excuse will persuade you to ditch your daily goal. As you build up this incredible power of commitment, incredible things will start happening for you.

- Every day is a chance to review and re-orientate where you are with your goal list. By reminding yourself where you are headed, each day will feel like a victory. Also take the time to celebrate when you achieve your scheduled goals. You have an abundance of strong points, and they should be celebrated.

- Affirmations can motivate you, like "I am unstoppable today." Seeing yourself as an unstoppable force that is working hard towards your next big goal is a benefit. You are, after all, the instrument of your own destiny. When obstacles arise, you crush them. When distractions happen, you refocus and keep working!

- Understand that lack of motivation breeds lack of motivation. Distraction leads to more distraction. You have to become like an iron fort that sets your time very carefully. When you have scheduled time to work, then work. Take regular breaks and make sure that you rest enough. But work time is work time—that is a rule.

- Learn how to stay focused[59] for extended periods of time. Focus is a skill, and you can learn how to hone yours. Everyone gets bored working toward their goals. This is when your creative side needs to jump in and mix things up. Do tomorrow's schedule today, scrap the schedule, and start over. Do something different, but stay motivated.

Self-motivation is driven by actions. If you find that you have stalled, take action! This is the only thing that can reenergize you and keep you on track.

Name five distractions that keep you from working. Record them here:

1.

2.

3.

4.

5.

---

59 James Clear, The Myth of Passion and Motivation: How to Stay Focused When You Get Bored Working Towards Your Goals, https://blog.bufferapp.com/the-myth-of-passion-and-motivation-how-to-stay-focused-when-you-get-bored-working-toward-your-goals

Practicing What You Preach: Tips

I can motivate[60] myself to do anything I want. It is a skill that I harnessed and have practiced since I was a young child. I saw others around me "taking it easy," and noticing the difference quickly adding up as time went on. In order to get to where you want to be, you have to put in the work!

So if you find yourself sitting down to begin work, but your phone beeps, or a friend pops round, or you check your social media status, or you send an email—remember this: the only way to get ahead with motivation is to keep at it. That means doing the thing that you should be doing, not something else. Here are tips to help you practice what you preach.

- *Focus all of your energy around your goal.* If you have a paper to write but you just cannot get started, perhaps planning is the issue. Work on planning a better paper. If you cannot do that, work on the idea behind the paper—maybe it is not inspiring you enough. If that is not the case, try writing the end first. Whatever you do, *do something*.

- *Time division makes people look like superheroes.* If you are excellent at managing your time, you can divide large projects into smaller chunks and get them done in tiny pieces. You do not have to write that paper in one day. If you know that you cannot sit for longer than three hours, plan to write every day for four days. You will end up with a polished, amazing paper with time to spare.

- *Practice your positive attitude.* If you hate your paper's topic or the writing you have done, then you need an attitude adjustment. Switch from working for a bit to improving your positive attitude. Put some upbeat music on and dance

---

60   Siimon Reynolds, How to Stay Super Motivated, http://www.forbes.com/sites/siimonreynolds/2013/07/28/how-to-stay-super-motivated/

around or accomplish something else quickly and efficiently, but improve your mood.

- *Ask your mentor for help.* Whether at school or at work, your mentor is there to help motivate you. If you just cannot do it, call them and express your issue. They will talk you through it and give you valuable advice. Sometimes you need to be told, "Hey, you have only had three hours of sleep in two days; maybe that is your problem."

- *Practice your visualization skills.* When you can see the outcome of your efforts in your mind's eye, you can keep yourself working. This works both ways; imagine the positive and negative side of things. If you do not do your paper correctly, you face a bad grade. If you do it brilliantly, you face praise and will feel proud of yourself.

- *Make sure you have the body basics covered.* You need to eat well, you need to sleep often, and you need to exercise. If your body does not function, neither will your brain or your motivation centers. Lasting energy comes from consistent health and wellness.

- *Dress for success, and wait for rewards.* Dressing up makes you feel good about yourself and can improve your mood. Even if you are not going anywhere, I urge you to get up, shower, and get dressed up anyway—it makes you feel great! Then do not forget to reward your own hard work. Take a day and enjoy the heck out of it.

What Greatness Means to You

Can you define greatness—the type that you know lives inside you? I believe that everyone has their own special brand of greatness, whether it is to be a leader, a mentor, an inventor, or an amazing architect. Each person in this world has unique gifts that they can use to bless others. I have a passion for helping others discover this in themselves.

So think of greatness[61] in this way—what distinguishes you from other people? How could you use this to further your own passions and help your family or community? Only you have the power to see inside your own heart. Greatness means different things to different people because we all have unique goals.

To a mother of three, it might mean the ability to send her kids to the best private or Ivy League schools one day. To someone else, it might mean the ability to create a unique and popular work of art. Greatness is memorable because it took a long time to achieve. There were trials, and there were tribulations and struggles. Few people are great in this day and age.

I want you to decide what greatness means to you by looking at the following concepts and allowing them to become internalized. Think about what they mean to you:

- *Greatness means awareness.* You know anything is possible and that your goals are within your reach. That has never been the issue. The issue has always been knowing how then doing it for long enough to make it a success.

- *Greatness is a process.* Personal evolution does not happen overnight. You cannot expect to be great today or tomorrow; it is a long-term goal. Defining your greatness and working towards it will get you closer than anyone else.

- *Greatness means shifting.* What you are doing now may not be good enough and may not make you happy. To be great, you need to go through a lot of difficult changes, but they are for the best. Prepare for a shift because you need it.

- *Greatness means failure.* Anyone in the world who has ever been great has failed over and over again. With greatness comes failure, but the more you fail, the more you learn. If you stop failing, you have stopped trying.

---

61 Barrie Davenport, 25 Ways to Become The Best Version of Yourself, http://liveboldandbloom.com/05/life-coaching/25-ways-to-become-the-best-version-of-yourself

- *Greatness[62] means values.* All great people have a key set of values that you admire. You should take note of these and nurture them inside yourself. You have the power to shape your personality and become a better version of yourself.

- *Greatness means vision.* There will be hard days, and there will be long days. There will be days when your plans seem futile. You must be true to the vision of the future that you have for yourself. That is the only truth you need.

- *Greatness means priorities.* Your focus, time, energy, and resources need to be on the right things, or greatness will never happen. Spend time where it should be spent, and do not allow unimportant things to hamper your progress.

What makes you great? Record it here:

_____

_____

_____

_____

_____

_____

---

62   Preston Waters, The Definition of Greatness, http://elitedaily.com/life/motivation/definition-greatness/

Being the Best Version of Yourself

The truth is tough to process once you let it sink in. Chances are you have to become the best version of yourself in order to achieve your life goals. This is true for most ambitious people, and it takes a lot of time and effort to get right. The good news is that being the best version of yourself is a noble goal, and it is something to live by.

You are now consciously building yourself into the person that you want to become. That much is clear, so whether you work hard or mess around, this will eventually become who you are. Our time here is limited and unknown. It is a scary thing to grasp, but that is why I prefer to work hard and make sure that I am becoming the best version of myself that is possible in the world.

People that are genuinely happy and successful are that way because these have met their goals. No one is happy or successful by mistake; both require a lot of work and energy. If you are quite lazy right now—and that serves no purpose in your life— cast it off. Your new main goal is to become a highly motivated, productive, hard-working person.

Do it enough and you will eventually embody that lifestyle. Your unique mix of traits and skills will make you who you are, but you will still want the most from each of these. It was Steve Jobs[63] that said, "Don't let the noise of others' opinions drown out your own inner voice." He meant that you should not allow other people to dictate your path in life.

If you are a young adult who is coming from an underprivileged background, then obstacles are much harder to overcome. There are hurdles that others may never have to experience, but you can use this to your advantage. The resilience that comes with the journey will help you excel in life, and it is so important for you

---

63 Steve Tobak, How to Be the Best Version of You, http://www.inc.com/steve-tobak/how-to-be-the-best-version-of-you.html

to do it. With every one of us that succeeds, the more youth that come after us will believe in it for themselves too.

When you work towards being the best version of yourself, regret vanishes. You know that you have been using your time for a worthy cause. You know that you are making yourself happy by being true to what you want and who you can be. This is perhaps the greatest thing that anyone can do for themselves in this life.

Society is shaped around mindless distraction, but it comes at a terrible price. With every day of meaningless use of your time, you allow time out of your life to be wasted—time that could be spent making things better for your family and for yourself. No one is going to do it for you. Either you rise to this calling or you slink back into the gentle hum of media distraction.

This is the only life that you get. You had better make the most of it!

Identify instances when you need to be motivated in your life:

_____

_____

_____

_____

_____

_____

_____

_____

_____

List key methods of motivating yourself:

_____

_____

_____

_____

_____

_____

_____

_____

CHAPTER 9

Working With Action Despite Inaction

"Remember, a real decision is measured by the fact that you've taken new action. If there's no action, you haven't truly decided."
Anthony Robbins

Inaction is all around us and easy to spot. Do not get me wrong; there is a lot of busy-ness, along with dreaming, but it is harder to find positive action towards set goals.

The key here is to learn to work with action, despite inaction—because it is always going to be there. Your mind and the outside world will try to lure you away from your goals over and over again. That is why this is the road less travelled—because it requires serious commitment. In this chapter, I will show you how to stay on your path.

The Real Secret of Success

What is the real secret of success that seems to elude so many people? On the May 15, 2011, I achieved my biggest accomplishment to date. I received my Bachelor's degree in engineering with a minor in African-American studies from Smith College. I had an awesome job opportunity waiting for me, and my career launch was on the horizon. It was the success I had been working towards for years.

Along the way there were so many obstacles and distractions that tried to pull me off my path and take me from my goals. I only managed to avoid them because of my constant focus. The incremental steps I had put in place made way for the inevitable outcome—graduation and the chance to succeed with an excellent degree behind my name.

There were many times when the door cracked open just a little bit, just like it did when I was a child. It was my job to decide whether or not to go for it. I had learned that pursuing goals was a risky business, but the rewards far outweighed the risks. I began my career as a Junior Project Manager at an Information Technology company in western Massachusetts reporting directly to the CEO.

I could not rely on returning home, so I had to make sure I had a career opportunity and living details settled before graduation. As an undergrad, during my visits home to Boston, I would survive home for maybe a day before my father would kick me out of my mother's house, and I had to figure out the rest of my stay. My visits home ended up becoming less and less frequent, and it took a toll on me emotionally while I kept putting it to the side with everything else I had going on. By the time it was my senior year, I created a plan to get as much exposure and attention for career opportunities before graduation as possible. Within a few weeks, I stood in front of my future employer.

I researched him in advance, prepared questions, and did my due diligence to show how hungry I was for an opportunity. The interview questions came as a surprise as they were more psychology-based vs. technical, with the first one being, "What are the three most important things about yourself?" but it was a fascinating process to test flexibility and quick thinking. As our interview went on, he seemed more and more impressed by my story and created a position for me on the spot to report directly to him.

I was floored! I thought of all the possibilities that came with flying under the wing of a CEO. How often do youth get a wedge open to start like this?

Success was my only option in this case, and I made it. When there is no room for error, no other choice but to succeed, you find a way. Before I had even walked across the stage for my degree, I had an amazing opportunity waiting for me. The real secret was that I planned it—then I *went* for it.

Activating Your Positive Mind

The jury is in—when you think positively about things, it helps you build your skillsets, improves your health, and helps you work more effectively. Being positive is not just a pleasant side effect of "having a good day" anymore. It is a critical brain function for setting the correct climate for personal development, growth, and the pursuit of knowledge.

That is why activating your positive mind[64] has become so important. Without positivity, I would never have made it through those insane study days at Smith or nailed the interview. Your future is like a house of cards—just one incorrect element interferes with your goal, and it could all come crashing down. More often than not, the element that interferes is within us—the negative mind.

Controlling and eliminating your negative thought patterns is instrumental to your development as someone who wants to succeed in this world. Science has already proven that positive thinking does more than create happiness; it actually forces you towards positive outcomes. Negativity attracts more negativity, so the same will apply for positivity.

64 James Clear, How Positive Thinking Builds Your Skills, Boots Your Health, and Improves Your Work, http://jamesclear.com/positive-thinking

Create five reminder affirmations to think more positively. Record them here:

1. _____

_____

2. _____

_____

3. _____

_____

4. _____

_____

5. _____

_____

A negative mind fires off chemical signals that narrow your frame of view. The outside world becomes limited, and your options become restricted. You have a lot of work to do, so you do not do any of it. Sound familiar? Positive thoughts, however, have been proven to open up the brain and inspire action. You will have more ideas and options as your world gets bigger.

This will be a challenge for you because the human brain[65] evolved to focus on negative thoughts. Back then, it would keep us from day-to-day threats and hazards. It would help us survive. These days, however, it just inspires negativity bias in everything that we do. You have to actively work on being a positive thinker in order to be one.

---

65 Julie Beck, How to Build a Happier Brain, http://www.theatlantic.com/health/archive/2013/10/how-to-build-a-happier-brain/280752/

Yes, you heard me! You need to actively practice positive thinking in your conscious mind if you are going to retrain your brain to see the opportunity in life. To activate your positive mind, you therefore need to include a list of practices into your daily regimen that will remind you to think in a more positive manner. Believe me, this works!

To keep your positive mind activated, you can also try to spend more time with positive people; negative people tend to have the opposite impact. Take responsibility in your life, and contribute to your community; this is also important. Continue to read and consume inspiring, positive material and media. Goal achievement creates a positive outlook.

Finally, you will have to recognize and actively replace negative thoughts with positive ones. When you catch yourself thinking something negative, stop. Reframe your perspective, and use a positive thought instead. Do this enough, and soon you will see the perspective shift.

The Growing Art of Persistence

Without fail, one of the most prized traits in successful people is persistence. It takes enormous persistence to succeed in anything most people would consider "great" or "beyond the norm." Look at Thomas Edison! He tried to invent the light bulb 10,000 times before he got it right. Most people would never have made it past their third attempt.

The only difference between an average person and Thomas Edison is that Edison knew persistence pays off. Persistence is the greatest teacher that you will ever have. With every failed attempt at something, you learn a little more and inch a little closer to success. If you refuse to give up but continue to learn, grow, and allocate time to the project, it will succeed.

Persistence is a trait that you must adopt if you are going to be successful. Prepare for failure, and change your mindset about it. Experience is the best teacher in life, and failures are a great opportunity to have a learning moment. It is up to you to bounce back and keep going despite the hardships, distractions, and failures that spring up around you. It is better to climb over these obstacles than to run away from them.

The first step to becoming more persistent is easy. Always assume that whatever you are doing is going to take more time[66] than you expect. Good things take a long time, and great things take a really long time. Instant success is an easy thing to get fooled by, but remember that when something sounds too good to be true, it probably is. It takes years to achieve long-term goals; the road is not well paved, but it will feel great when you achieve those milestones.

The next step is understanding that failure is just a word and idea that has gained a lot of bad weight. The idea of failing is not something bad if you have the right mindset about it. Do not allow the word to set you up to quit on your wishes and goals. Failure comes with the territory of your success plan.

Once you have reined in your thoughts, allocated enough time, and reframed how you see failure, the only thing left is to keep your stress levels low. Emotions can cause shifts in moods and perspective, and these can knock you off course. Stress tends to do it best. Be mindful of your stress levels, and actively work to keep them in check.

Remember, all of these are active responses to the negative results built up over time. Once you realize your stress is too high, I urge you to stop and make your game plan to get back on track and lower the level. It will help you focus and stay on track. Do not give room for inaction as it would mean accepting failure in a negative way, internalizing it, and feeling bad about how awful you are for weeks, maybe years. Your ability to persist creates a stronger, resilient individual.

---

66 Donald Latumahina, 7 Sure-Fire Ways to Develop Persistence, http://www.lifeoptimizer.org/2007/11/19/7-sure-fire-ways-to-develop-persistence/

Change your last five failures into learning opportunities. What would the successful outcomes have been? Record them here:

1. _____

2. _____

3. _____

4. _____

5. _____

Working With Intense Emotions

Emotional intensity[67] has been scientifically proven to impact your perception and the way that you think. It has been shown that people with intense emotions seek out variety, novelty, and complexity. They also tend to work harder and have stronger desires to achieve success. Of course, when your emotions are heightened, productivity bottoms out.

While growing up, I had many situations where my emotions would run high. This came from the dysfunction of a traumatic

---

67   Daniel Goleman, Intensity of Emotion Tied to Perception and Thinking, http://www.nytimes.com/1987/03/17/science/intensity-of-emotion-tied-to-perception-and-thinking.html

childhood. If you have dealt with difficult moments growing up, then you will also need to learn to cope with difficult emotions so that they do not hamper your progress in life.

Repressed emotion usually results in intense, uncontrolled emotion that manifests because of fear. When this happens, it becomes overwhelming, and you lose touch with reality. This is when you need to take time to work through your emotions. Do not ignore them! Extremely painful emotions will simply cause grief, anger, and outbursts if left repressed.

There are three main techniques[68] that you can use to re-orientate when these emotions strike. Use these techniques to refocus and continue along your destined path:

- *Grounding*: Also known as "centering," this helps you bring your awareness into the present moment. Physically, it helps you reduce and release stress and tension. Mentally, you reclaim your focus on imagined or past events and focus more on the present. Relaxed breathing and triangular breathing are examples of grounding.

- *Mindful walking*: This can be done any time, wherever you are. Stand and intentionally relax your body, starting with your upper body, your head, your neck, and your jaw. Focus your eyes on the ground a few feet ahead of you, and take in the sensations around you as you walk.

- *Awareness of surroundings*: Another grounding technique can be done at home. Take off your shoes, and place both feet on the ground where you are sitting. Place your hands on your lap. Focus on light breathing, and pay attention to the sounds and smells around you. You will need to be in a peaceful place for this one.

---

68   Glen Rowe, How to Regulate Intense Emotions, http://www.bellwood.ca/files/articles/How_to_Regulate_Intense_Emotions_1305554948.pdf

> **Name three instances when emotions have derailed your work ethic lately. Record them here:**
>
> 1. _____
>
>   _____
>
> 2. _____
>
>   _____
>
> 3. _____
>
>   _____

Grounding can be a very useful tool to defuse your emotions. Take note that these techniques will not work if the source of conflict is still around. You will have to be alone so that you can refocus and reframe your internal experience.

How to Recover From Emotional Turmoil

Emotional turmoil is traumatic, and while people do not refer to it like this, it leaves scars anyway. If you have suffered through years of emotional trauma as a child, you will no doubt be suffering from some as an adult. Recovering from these experiences is very important if you are going to move ahead with your life and make a success of it.

People react differently to emotional turmoil depending on their past and the coping skills that they have developed for it. There are three key phases[69] that you need to work through to

---

69   Phases of Traumatic Recovery, http://trauma-recovery.ca/recovery/phases-of-trauma-recovery/

recover from emotional turmoil. Take note of these, and use them as needed:

- *Phase 1 – Safety and stabilization*: Find out what the root trauma is, and commit to work on it. These emotional traumas cause a ripple effect in everyday life, which leads to runaway emotions in seemingly unimportant situations. Learn to regulate your present emotions using grounding, and consider finding a therapist or, at minimum, a trusted person in your life to open up to. Make sure that you are in safe surroundings with people that you trust when they get the better of you.

- *Phase 2 – Remembrance and mourning*: Focus on working on your emotional trauma from the past. Speak to a counselor or psychologist, or engage in group therapy. Consider finding a safe way for expression and release, such as journaling or painting. The point is to release negative emotions here, not to relive the trauma. If it still hurts you too much, revert to phase 1. Understand what causes your emotional turmoil and outbursts, and work on it. Pay attention to any emotional pain in the present moment, and understand that it might be distorted. Gaining awareness that your reactions may be disproportionate is key here. Reduce your stress levels by practicing the re-grounding, mindfulness, and awareness techniques we talked about earlier.

- *Phase 3 – Reconnection and integration*: A new sense of self and a new future must be recognized in this phase. Healing and growing means redefining who you are and helping others. The trauma will no longer hold power over your life, because you have learned to let it go. Emotional trauma[70] takes time to heal and leaves people in its wake.

---

70 Traumatic Stress, http://www.helpguide.org/articles/ptsd-trauma/traumatic-stress.htm

Taking on more guilt will not help you. Give yourself the chance to heal by practicing self-compassion. You have been through a lot and are trying to recover. Release your anxiety, let go of depression, and embrace the healing phases.

Recovering from emotional turmoil can take a few weeks or a few years. The more you work on it and are aware of it, the less it will impact your current state. When you are mindful like this and can ground yourself in the present, you will be able to refocus on your goals and stick to your schedule no matter what happens. It will not be easy, but you will get better at it.

List the last three times you experienced raw emotional turmoil. Record them here:

1. _____

_____

2. _____

_____

3. _____

_____

The "Side Step" Rule of Three

There are a set of rules that I have adhered to over the years that have been tremendously helpful when emotions flair and threaten to set me back with my goals. Remember, you will never be able to succeed if these emotions keep interfering with your life. You have to learn to get them under control so that your plans will come to fruition.

I like to call this set of rules the "side step" rule of three because it helps you side step the emotional turmoil that results after something or someone has triggered you. Actively stopping this process[71] requires some serious clarity, so once you have regained your situational awareness, the next step is to stick to the rules.

Rule #1: Release Rejection and Do Not Brood

When someone rejects you, it activates the same pathways in your brain that cause physical pain. Needless to say, it hurts on a lot of levels. Feeling rejected messes with your ability to think, to recall memories, and to make good decisions—so you need to let it go. That means you may not, under any circumstances, dwell on things. No brooding at all.

Rule #2: Your Self-Esteem Is Bullet Proof

Failure is a positive step towards your future, albeit a painful one. If you view failures positively, your self-esteem may not internalize them and you may not feel bad about yourself. Do your best, learn from your mistakes, and let go of blame. You only have a certain amount of control with any situation, assignment, or project. Forgive your mistakes, and treasure your self-esteem.

Rule #3: Guilt Is Only Allowed as a Preventative Measure

Guilt and shame can be killers, especially if you have convinced yourself that everything is your fault. You need to make sure that guilt is only a useful emotion when it prevents you from hurting someone or making another mistake. Otherwise random feelings of guilt are not allowed. If you have apologized, you have no right to feel guilty anymore. Let it go.

If you use these three rules, you will be able to let go of most negative emotional circumstances, and this will keep you on track.

---

71 Dr. Mercola, 5 Tips for Recovering From Emotional Pain, http://articles.mercola. com/sites/articles/archive/2013/08/15/emotional-pain-recovery-tips.aspx

You can also try a technique called the "Emotional Freedom Technique," which uses tapping along specific energy meridians on your body to free blocked emotions and help you get past the way you are feeling.

Keep in mind that a lot of emotional turmoil gets worse when you allow your stress levels to become unmanageable. Learning how to release stress is key to maintaining a healthy emotional balance.

Use the side step rule of three to stop emotional pain in its tracks. First ground yourself, then practice awareness, then use the rule of three to put everything back in context. If you do this, you will be able to gather your senses and continue along your path.

Describe an instance where you became emotional, and detail how you could have stopped it using the methods described in this chapter.

List the main methods that are useful in defusing emotional pain:

_____

_____

_____

_____

_____

_____

_____

_____

GROWTH: WHEN DO YOU ACHIEVE YOUR DREAMS?

CHAPTER 10

Growing Into Your Dreams

"Keep your dreams alive. Understand to achieve anything requires faith and belief in yourself, vision, hard work, determination, and dedication. Remember all things are possible for those who believe."
Gail Devers

Everyone has dreams, and dream achievement is a long-term concept, which is why so few people are able to get there. The secret is to grow into your dreams. As you learn and your knowledge base expands, your dreams will become more specific; they will change and evolve like clouds taking shape in the sky.

If you stay on your path and stick closely to your goals, you will eventually grow into your dreams. Before you know it, you will have new dreams because you will be living the ones you had as a child and a young person. Dreams help you reach for higher goals—higher than most people dare to go. But they are waiting for you.

The Corporate America Chronicles

When I was a little girl, I would wish myself away from home and dream of my future life intensely—from having my own place, to starting my own business, to giving back to my community, to even the smallest details, like having my own puppy. I never lost sight of what I wanted to grow into. Years later, I was realizing that my dreams were now coming into existence as I graduated and began a full-time career. The corporate environment was not new to me as I had summer internships and a full year of design clinic for engineering, so I knew that it was to my advantage to be a sponge. I observed, took notes, and applied everything I could when I was around the Chief Executive Officer (CEO) to see how ideas were planned, communicated, and implemented across the enterprise and how so many factors are in play from change management to organizational culture.

I transitioned to working with the Executive Vice President/ Chief Operating Officer (EVP/COO) of the organization about a year later and was promoted to a Technical Project Manager position. In this position, I interacted with all operational IT units, including network, systems, infrastructure, support, software development, and ecommerce. I was fascinated by my COO's leadership style. He was dynamic; his ability to recognize subtle cues in the environment to fine tune how he communicated to the enterprise overall was impressive and something I wanted to absorb and learn. He believed I was a high potential employee and always fed my curiosity and hunger with challenges.

I viewed all of my leaders back then as mentors and found that as long as I stayed hungry, they were going to keep feeding me that valuable experience I needed to get ahead of the pack. The lesson here is that with the right perspective, anything is possible. With any offered opportunity, there is a choice. How you see it and what you do with it is what matters most.

It was early in 2014 that I was fully comfortable and settled into my new life in Western MA. I had secured almost three years with my first professional employer and had been living on my own for about seven years. I kept waking up and feeling like I was on cruise control and that I was not living my dream just yet.

At the time, my employer had new opportunities out in the Pacific Northwest of the United States to work with our biggest client for three years. I went through rounds of interviews and even took a trip out to Boise, Idaho, where I would relocate to, met wonderful people out there, and even tried envisioning what the whole experience would feel like. They even offered a company car and cell phone as part of the package.

I was at a crossroads again, where I needed to decide (quickly) whether or not I would commit the next three years (minimum) of my life out there. I knew that I could take the safe, reliable choice and take the promotion out West, but it did not feel right in my gut. I spent every day trying to figure out how I could make the move to Boise work—planning trips I would take to explore the U.S., figuring out in my calendar when I could see my family and friends again, and more. Something in my gut was just telling me this was not in alignment with my dreams, and it hit me every time I reflected on the vacations I had taken over the past few years to Southern California.

I had a burning desire to take a leap and explore either Southern California or Miami (I traveled once for a National Hispana Leadership Institute conference my senior year with Smith Nosotras members), where I would have to really figure everything out and start fresh. The idea of moving across the country in either direction was a pipe dream. It sounded great in my head but very difficult to actually achieve in the time frame I was working with. I felt like my engineering degree was being underutilized, and this still bothered me.

I was learning a ton, such as finding my own leadership style at work and learning how to fine tune my approach to get the most effective results within a team setting, and overall genuinely having a great time with my team, but a void was growing inside my heart. Shockingly to the business, I turned down the promotion to Boise and knew I had a new dream I would have to pursue. Sometimes you have to listen to the desires of your heart and just go for it.

Daring to Take the Next Big Step

You are on the edge of something big—you can feel it. However, where there is a cliff, there is also a drop off. Take one wrong step and you could end up plummeting into the abyss, right? Well, that is how most people feel about their dreams. That although these dreams would be incredible, there is simply too much risk, hard work, and "magic" required to get there. That is why big dreamers are courageous people—they have to be.

It takes real courage to turn your dreams into a reality. What most people do not recognize is that dreams need to be broken down into stages. You need to *earn* your dream. In other words, the thing that needs the most work is you. I would never have found financial freedom and independence if I did not actively define my success, learn what that meant, and take the action steps I needed to take to get there.

It took 16 years to get my undergraduate degree. Within that time, I had an abundance of learning moments through hard lessons of life to fight through. The dreams were always the same; it was I that needed to evolve and grow. I had to learn how to earn my dreams. That is why when you dare to take the next big step on your road to success, you will know it is coming.

You would have been working towards it all along. Dreams are not windfalls, and they do not happen by accident. Dreams are simply well executed plans combined with persistence and a willingness to never let go of what you want out of life.

List five dreams that you have had about your future recently. Record them here:

1. _____

_____

2. _____

_____

3. _____

_____

4. _____

_____

5. _____

_____

I am speaking about lifestyle dreams, the kind that tell you where you want to be in life. If, like me, you dreamed of not having to struggle financially, to live on your own, or to have a dream career, then that is a vivid dream that you should be actively working towards. The "G" part of the WEDGE system is all about learning to GROW into your dreams, like I grew into mine.

The only factor at this point that is preventing you from growing into your dreams is fear.[72] You do not believe it is possible, so you are too afraid to try. Your dream has already happened in your heart and mind. Now you need to believe that it can happen in your life. You need to cross the endless divide between fear and courage to make that happen.

---

72 Natalie Jesionka, How to (Finally!) Find the Courage to Pursue Your Dream, https://www.themuse.com/advice/how-to-finally-find-the-courage-to-pursue-your-dream

Begin by letting go of the doubt that you have. Of course you doubt your dream; you cannot achieve it right away! You have to work through many different phases first. Doubt feeds fear, and that is holding you back. Dare to say that it is possible. Then dare to create a plan that will make sure that it happens—even if that plan takes 20 years!

How Attitude Determines Your Perspective

That same perspective that was keeping you from starting down that dream path has impacted you in other areas too. It all stems back to your attitude and the way that you interact with the world. It is a simple truth in life that your attitude determines how far you will go. A good attitude will take you anywhere; a bad attitude will keep you frozen and inactive.

The great thing is that attitude is a choice. The attitude that you have now has determined where you are. If you are in a good place, then you must have a good attitude. If you are in a bad place, then you have a bad attitude. Did you identify with what I just said? Now what if I told you that if you had a good attitude, it would not matter what you have or do not have?

You have to change your attitude and your perspective[73] if you are ever going to reach your dreams. Take this analogy as an example. There is a tall building; two people are looking at it from different perspectives. One feels hopeful and full of joy, while the other feels miserable and full of doubt. But they are both looking at the same building. How can this be?

The first person is standing at the entrance looking up. They see a tall, magnificent building and dream about reaching the top of their field. The other person is at the top of the building looking down to the ground and sees a high, scary drop down. The subject is the same, but the way the two people perceive it is completely different.

---

73 How Your Perspective Affects Your Attitude, http://ownyourambition.com/how-your-perspective-affects-your-attitude/

Write down how you feel about people, places, and the world. Record them here:

_____

_____

_____

_____

_____

_____

That is what perspective can do in your life. Most people are wired to see things negatively, which skews their interpretation on what is possible and what is not. A negative person would rather not try so that they do not have to fail. They do not even see that if they do try, and try, and try some more, they will succeed, and the rewards will be plentiful.

Your personal attitude[74] impacts how you treat other people and how you approach life; it is contagious and impacts our health. It is the reason why we have good or bad experiences. Most days are mundane; the same things happen. When you have a good day, it is because your perspective or attitude is better.

To change your attitude is to change your perspective on life. To do this, you must identify and understand what it is that you need to change. Look at your life right now and how you react to it. How should you be reacting to it? Then try to find a role model so that you can mirror their positive attitude about life.

---

74   Paige Burkes, Your Attitude Determines Your Outcome, http://www.simplemindfulness.com/2012/03/25/attitude-determines-outcome/

Growth Hacking Explained

There are two types of growth hacking; one is a term coined by marketing folk and is not what we are talking about here. Instead, we are taking a more literal approach to growth. The term "hacking" is a modern term for "finding the easiest route" or "the fastest, quickest method"—you see it being used all the time to describe cracking different codes in the tech industry.

In this instance, growth hacking refers to the act of finding the quickest, easiest method to obtaining consistent growth in your life. You are "hacking" the personal growth system to uncover how you can get the most out of growing into your dreams during your lifetime.

One of the most common problems with this formula is consistency. It is so easy to be bumped off your path or to veer off in another direction and forget about your core goals. We all grow into something, and if you are not growing in that direction, eventually you are not going to be actively pursuing anything worthwhile.

Some experts even say that the only formula worth using is that constant[75] discipline = personal growth. Without consistency, you let go of the main purpose behind your actions, and your goals become lost. Suddenly you are spending your time in the wrong places and focusing on things that will not benefit you in the long run.

There is a precarious balance here because you will have your long-term dreams and your short-term goals that coexist. Sometimes your short-term plans need to be more intensive, and they can crowd out your long-term dreams. Potty training a puppy, for example, can end up stealing weeks of your life.

---

75 Sean Moore, Consistent Discipline = Personal Growth, http://medexec.org/consistent-discipline-personal-growth/

Which areas of your life need growth so that you can achieve your dreams? Record them here:

While this is great for that day when he knows that he does his business on the grass outside, ultimately you have to decide whether investing four hours a day for three months was worth the long-term sacrifice. Financial security is a lofty dream but is totally achievable if you have a solid plan to work towards. I am not saying put your life on hold for it but rather make sure the bulk of your actions remain true to your ultimate calling. This will ensure that consistency is maintained.

Personal growth[76] requires consistency in order to remain functional, otherwise goals and dreams break down. Success does not happen overnight but rather through the tiny decision to keep working towards a goal for a long, long time. Behind consistency, there is a long list of things that you need to make sure that you are covering for yourself.

If you cannot look after this list, then a breakdown will naturally happen because you will not have the physical, mental, or emotional energy to keep at it.

76　The Only Consistent Secret for Personal Growth, http://sidsavara.com/personal-development/the-only-consistent-secret-for-personal-growth

The Six Laws of Consistent Personal Growth

In order to consistently reach for that growth that you need in order to achieve your dreams, you must be prepared to follow some laws. These rules will help keep you in check and will govern the growth process for you. Whatever happens, stick to these, and you will always come back to personal growth and resume chasing your dream.

Law #1: Personal growth is about purposeful intention.

Reaching a point where you become successful and achieve your dreams is only possible if you purposefully intend on getting there. You must, with all of your heart, want to get there and must plan accordingly. Intentions are driven by actions, and without a route forward, you cannot retain any kind of consistent behavior for personal growth.

Law #2: Personal growth is about personal value.

Stand in front of a mirror and recite what you see. This is you, and you are the driving force behind your dreams. You need to add value to yourself in order to achieve them, which means learning, growing, and going through hardships. You control your thoughts, decisions, and directions, so make sure they are always adding personal value to you.

Law #3: Personal growth is about climate.

You need to create a climate or environment for personal growth if you want to be able to achieve it consistently. That means setting yourself up for success internally and externally. Do not go out with your friends to the bar the night before you have an important exam or meeting the next morning. You decide where you are and how it works.

Law #4: Personal growth is about trial and error.

You will learn from many people on your journey and will have many mentors. Do not forget that you are an individual. You will discover your own unique processes, techniques, and systems for keeping yourself in line as you progress on this journey. Never simply trust the strategies of other people when your own can be much more powerful.

Law #5: Personal growth means becoming mature human beings.

You will have to grow in character along with skill so that you will be the kind of person that can shoulder the responsibility that comes with living your ultimate dream. That means being a mature person who cares, has integrity, and is concerned about others. Make sure that on your journey, you grow into a person of character.

Law #6: Personal growth means embracing change.

Change is going to happen, which means that what you have now is not what you will have later. You will have to be all right with making trade-offs and accepting big changes in your life. This will mean your relationships, your career, and your social circles may change. Remember that to stay motivated, you have to accept this and keep going.

The Lives I've Influenced (Interview Spotlight)

I have taught many people many things. In this interview spotlight, you will see the traits that stand out in me as told by the people closest to me.

Geovanny Interiano: Your presence. Even if you are unsure of yourself, you would never know it looking at you. You have a way of just looking comfortable and blending in to the background but also know how to command people's attention at the same time. It's incredible.

Zuleika Toribio: Your "I don't give a f***" attitude and your hard exterior while managing to maintain a soft and sincere heart. I've noticed that you are willing to do all that you can to make sure that those people you care about/loved ones are doing well whether it is financially, mentally, emotionally, or physically while at the same time protecting yourself and your emotions.

Krystal Cummings: What stands out most about Iris is how genuine and humble she is. She is dynamic in so many ways, but she is always her true self.

Cynthia V. Gomez S.: Your take on life is liberating. I come from a traditional Latino upbringing where it may feel restrictive at times, and your take on life is freeing because you are able to step back and recognize that you must go for what you want in life in order to be successful and happy.

Leba: Your perspective has changed and grown in the light of opportunity and hard work. That opportunities in life are part hard work and karma. That life is what you make it and that it is in your hands to control.

Michelle Restrepo: You're the "take the bull by its horns" kind of girl. What you say, you do. There are no ifs or buts, just whens. I absolutely admire that way of thinking since it can be very challenging to act on.

Stacy Diaz: Your ability to set goals and accomplish them. You had calendars and would map everything out. I remember your crazy calendar on your wall when you lived in Tyler.

Suly A.: Your incredible heart. You hold so much and yet today you are able to smile and let go of bitterness, little by little, because it's a process. Your self-reflection is amazing because you are able to recognize what is not working for you and then you make a plan to change it. Your mind is instantly made up that this is not right and you will no longer take part in it. You are inspiring because you can literally live with the poison around you yet you live what you preach. You remain STRONG.

Steve Flores: You are proactive and demonstrate an ability to be disciplined. When you took on the challenge of becoming healthier, I was so proud and inspired. You really committed and become an example of what it means to be disciplined and motivated. I think this permeates into your take on life. You don't allow yourself to get stuck; you really take the time to move forward and understand that at times there will be challenges along the way but truly learn from that challenge and obstacle and move forward.

Describe your life right now and what your dream life could be. How would you close the distance?

_____

_____

_____

_____

_____

Bullet point the dreams that mean the most to you here:

_____

_____

_____

_____

_____

CHAPTER 11

The Hack Attitude: How to Solve Problems

"A growth hacker is a person whose true north is growth. Everything they do is scrutinized by its potential impact on scalable growth."

Sean Ellis

As an engineer, I grew up constantly streamlining everything; it was the most natural process in the world to me. Yet as I moved through school and college, I realized that for many people, troubleshooting, finding answers, and seeking out solutions to problems was not something that everyone did of their own accord.

It became very clear that a lot of students simply did not have that "hack" attitude that was required to get to the bottom of a problem, especially if they were not instructed where to find the answers. I want you to succeed in your life, so I am going to share one of my own success secrets with you in this chapter—how to solve any problem.

What Is Hacking and Why Do You Need It?

Even with mentors, stepping into a new career fresh from college was a challenge. No one is there to help you with the finer details of orientation, and you have to work extremely hard to catch up on things like company culture, what their systems are, and how to use them best to your advantage. You run into a lot of problems that you have to solve yourself.

I did not have family members or school resources that worked in the corporate world to look towards for advice. What I had was a lifetime of situations that provided a space to solve problems and a new degree. As an engineer, I learned how to "hack" problems in college to get to the heart of the solution. You had to be able to tear an issue apart and reassemble it to understand things.

I developed a very keen process for problem solving, and it is a system that I still use every day. I have never shied away from challenges or obstacles, because I strip them down to their moving parts until I know enough to come up with a viable solution. I have always thought of this as my superpower, and in some ways, I have been doing it since I was a child.

Hacking, for me, means cracking the system. I believe that every problem or challenge has an ideal process that will result in an accurate answer or solution. When you have this kind of system on your side, you can solve any issue you face alone. This is a skill that you can bank on. It will be there for you when everyone else is busy.

Accessing Information the Easy Way

In today's world, we all have our own virtual assistant at our fingertips if we are fortunate to have Internet access. However, information alone is not knowledge. You have to know where to look, in what context you are searching, and how the information fits together according to any existing knowledge that you may possess. Not everything on the Internet is true; in fact, most of it is personal perspective.

> **How often do you actively search for solutions or answers whether online or through other primary resources?**
>
> _____
>
> _____
>
> _____
>
> _____
>
> _____
>
> _____

The Internet, however, really comes to life in the context of hacking of problems. By its very nature, hacking requires searching for answers, and the Internet can be a valuable tool in this process. It is there for you to use for in-depth research, and you should take advantage of it and find those golden primary resources. It would surprise you how few people scratch beneath the page one surface.

To access information[77] easily, all you have to do is search for the right term. Discovering the right term, however, will require a process of problem solving or hacking. Here is how I do it, and it always helps me arrive at the right answer. Remember, this process can be used for anything you are trying to solve for; primary resources may include the Internet, but that is just the surface.

---

77 Adam Dachis, A Systematic Approach to Solving Just About Any Problem, http://lifehacker.com/5795228/how-to-solve-just-about-any-problem

Step 1: Identify Your Problem

Here you will identify and recognize the issue as well as the nature of the issue, and you will seek definition for that issue. Take some time to write out the problem and define what you are actually trying to solve. All of this can be done online as you gather the correct language to use in your searches.

Step 2: Structure Your Problem

During this stage, you will figure out what you need to measure whether through observations, inspections, and any other data to collect and develop a clear idea of what the problem is and how it should be approached. Resources online will help you here.

Step 3: Solution Discovery

Once you understand the problem and what you are trying to solve, you will find a host of potential solutions with possible credible sources. Do not worry about evaluating them yet; right now you only want to focus on where or who the source is and if they are credible. Find several options. There are several tools online that you can find that help you research website reputations, or you can find scientific studies, journal publishes, and more that will help you in the discovery. Consider your physical world as well for solutions; books, people, and papers are also sources to consider.

Step 4: Decide via Process of Elimination

After your sources have been collected, analyze each of them for context, clarity, and relevance, and see if they provide the best possible solution to your problem. A blend of these could also work. Try working backwards by eliminating feeble sources first.

Step 5: Implement and Gain Feedback

The final stage will be testing out your solution to improve your own knowledge. Remember that the sources you find are based on other people's opinions or research, but they remain untested in your life. It is up to you to test them and gather feedback from your results.

Using Gratitude as a Guiding Principle

Problem solving is about more than simply searching for answers. It is also about being grateful for the people, places, and knowledge sources that you have at your disposal. Time and time again I have been lucky to move up in my career because of the people in my life. I firmly believe I am a product of the community of people who have helped to provide for, guide, and support me through life, and without them, I would not be where I am today. If you do not have an "attitude of gratitude," then you are approaching life incorrectly.

As you know, no one owes you anything. It is up to you to work hard and make your own way in this world. It is also up to you to nurture valuable relationships along the way and to maintain a positive attitude all the way through these tough challenges. Gratitude is the single most useful principle that has helped me succeed in my career.

First of all, it opens a lot of new doors for you. Being grateful and showing appreciation help you make and keep new friends in new environments. You would be surprised what an underutilized skill being grateful has become. Forbes[78] also recently reported that gratitude improves your physical health as you are more likely to look after yourself.

It has a lot of pleasant side effects too, like the fact that people who are grateful get better quality sleep, enjoy enhanced empathy and reduced aggression, and have improved self-esteem. My personal favorite boost from gratitude comes in the form of

---

78 Amy Morin, 7 Scientifically Proven Benefits of Gratitude That Will Motivate You to Give Thanks All Year Round, http://www.forbes.com/sites/amymorin/2014/11/23/7-scientifically-proven-benefits-of-gratitude-that-will-motivate-you-to-give-thanks-year-round/

mental strength. When you use it often, it drastically reduces your stress levels.

This, in turn, makes you a more resilient person, and resilience is something that you really need in a business environment. Experts have been talking about gratitude for a long time, and they have found through various investigations and studies that gratitude is one of the most important factors in a person's overall happiness.

What are you grateful for in your life? Record it here:

When you practice gratitude[79] as your guiding principle, it makes you a more balanced person. You learn to openly appreciate your life and everything in it. Emotionally, you feel better; personally, you become a nicer person; career-wise, it improves your networking skills and decision-making ability; and health-wise, it boosts your energy levels.

I can honestly say that if I did not live according to this principle, I would not be where I am now. People care when you care, and gratitude is a vital element in the process. Strengthen

---

79 Amit Amin, The 31 Benefits of Gratitude You Didn't Know About: How Gratitude Can Change Your Life, http://happierhuman.com/benefits-of-gratitude/

yourself by adopting this guiding principle and practicing in your own life.

The Power of a Positive Attitude

I will never forget hearing that "your attitude determines your altitude" for the first time. I thought it was very catchy and wanted to know more. What I discovered was that the statement was very true; your attitude really does determine how far you get in this life. A positive attitude in particular is a very powerful ally to have on your side.

As a problem solver, you will need a positive attitude[80] along with gratitude in order to solve problems. Hacking a situation might be a long and tedious process, so being able to stay on track with your pursuit for the answer is half of the solution.

Just look at the things that the average person has to face on a daily basis. We become consumed with worry, we are afraid of situations or people, we can blame others when things do not go as planned, we may complain, we may criticize, and we may generate mistrust or become jealous. Sometimes all of these things can happen before your morning cup of coffee.

With so many challenges as part of your average business day, you have to nurture a positive attitude to combat these negative emotions, or they will drain you. You will never have the energy to find solutions to your problems in your own time if you are preoccupied with trivial, negative feelings floating around the office.

Having a "glass half full" attitude will make you more resilient, which is what you need. Working environments are competitive and, more, they can be cutthroat. By resisting negative thinking and actively adopting a positive attitude, you will have more energy, and you will be able to inspire other people every day.

---

80 Frank Sonnenberg, The Power of a Positive Attitude, http://www.franksonnenbergonline.com/blog/the-power-of-a-positive-attitude/

Plus being positive[81] decreases your stress levels, has physical and psychological benefits, makes you live longer, and helps you cope during difficult times. You will need this attitude as you adjust to new jobs and new people. I also mentioned previously that being positive helps you focus, which means that skill building becomes easier.

When you are constantly in a positive frame of mind, good things will happen for you. Not only will you become a more stable person but you will begin to enjoy everything that you do with more vigor. Take it from me; this is one trait that you want in your life.

When You Came From Nothing

Problem solving as an adult has a formula that you simply did not have as a young person living with such extreme adversity. When you came from nothing, you will always have that drive inside you to be more. Harness it! I have met some incredible people that have grown into the most amazing examples of what happens when drive meets problem solving ability. I am even more fortunate to call many of these people friends and family. My aim is to add your story here.

To recap, in order to become a growth hacker and dial in to new places and people, you will have to learn how to hack the system. That means applying a problem solving formula and having a gracious heart and a positive attitude. If you can add these to the drive that you have to be better, nothing will be able to stop you!

I love the saying "when you come from nothing, anything is possible." You are a blank slate, and the world is waiting for your gifts. When you have come from an "at-risk" background and you have been told your entire life that you will never amount to

---

81 James Clear, The Science of Positive Thinking: How Positive Thoughts Build Your Skills, Boost Your Health, and Improve Your Work, http://www.huffingtonpost.com/james-clear/positive-thinking_b_3512202.html

> **Write down all the things you wanted as a child but never had. Record them here:**
>
> _____
>
> _____
>
> _____
>
> _____
>
> _____
>
> _____

anything, you have absolutely nowhere to go but up. How high you go depends on you.

Your ultimate dream might be to own your own practice, open up a community center, or work at a Fortune 500 company. It might be to travel often or to live on a beach somewhere with your family. Whatever your dream, growing into it is going to take everything you have—including your own ability to hack your way through the obstacles that you face.

To some, coming from nothing[82] might be seen as a disadvantage, but I realized that it was an advantage. I worked harder than other people. I wanted it more than they did. I turned my hunger into a strength thanks to my evolving attitude and problem solving skills. I will never forget connecting with my first mentor CEO over common ground.

---

82 Gurbaksh Chahal, When You Come From Nothing Anything Is Possible: How I Was Able to Live 'The Dream', http://elitedaily.com/money/when-you-come-from-nothing-anything-is-possible-how-i-was-able-to-live-the-dream/

"You can do anything that you put your mind to" is something my mother always told me when I was growing up, and you must—or you will regret it forever. With these problem solving skills, there is nothing you cannot do, and that is the truth. Twenty years ago people did not have the Internet to help them, but you do. Use it wisely, and make a life for yourself.

How to Revamp Your Upbringing

Let's be honest here; your upbringing was less than ideal. So many things could have been better, but they were not. This is in your past now, but it is still a part of who you are. I found that when I started to rise and reach my full potential, I had to revamp my upbringing and relearn vital skills that I was never taught. You may find that you have to do the same.

Be a creator in your life, and challenge the victim mentality. We know that there are systematic and institutional issues[83] working against those that come from poor backgrounds (and in some cases, hold them in place[84]), but there is still a fight in us. The good news is that now you are older; you are in control and can change it. Channel your energy and mindset into how you can achieve what you want—period.

Revamping your upbringing means exposing yourself to people that learn from and build with. These people will create environments in which you can openly be yourself and share conversations. You can share experiences with them to grow your perspective and understanding of the world around you.

Accept within yourself that not everyone that is around you truly wants you to succeed. Home will always be a part of you,

83   Richard V. Reeves, The Other American Dream: Social Mobility, Race and Opportunity, http://www.brookings.edu/blogs/social-mobility-memos/posts/2013/08/28-social-mobility-race-opportunity-reeves

84   Michelle Chen, Moving On Up and Hitting a Wall: Social Mobility in the U.S. and Europe, http://www.commondreams.org/views/2010/02/11/moving-and-hitting-wall-social-mobility-us-and-europe

but it might mean you may have to create some distance so that it does not continue to control you and bring you down. Sometimes people pretend to be supportive, but they do not mean it. They know if you succeed you will leave them behind. Be wary of that!

Revamping your upbringing[85] is all about experience. The more you can get out there into the real world, the more you can learn. I learned so much from my first few weeks at work, things that I thought I knew but could not really understand until I was there.

As you move through your various experiences, take it all in. Accept that this is who you are now and that you are no longer that helpless child who could not escape their circumstances. Make a conscious decision to keep learning and growing as a human being so that you level up and get to where you need to go.

Name five things in childhood you wish you could change. Then let them go!

1. _____

2. _____

3. _____

4. _____

5. _____

---

85 Tracy McMillan, 7 Best Pieces of Advice for People Who Want to Move Past a Rotten Childhood, http://www.oprah.com/relationships/7-Best-Pieces-of-Advice-for-People-Who-Want-to-Move-Past-a-Rotten-Childhood

Describe the most efficient way to solve a problem in your life.

_____

_____

_____

_____

_____

_____

Create a bullet point list of the problem-solving process:

_____

_____

_____

_____

_____

_____

---- CHAPTER 12 ----

The Five Phases of Growth Success

"Those who improve with age embrace the power of personal growth and personal achievement and begin to replace youth with wisdom, innocence with understanding, and lack of purpose with self-actualization."
Bo Bennett

Personal growth happens whether you facilitate it or not. It can happen quickly or slowly, and if you are not careful, you could become something that you do not like. That is why playing an active role in the success of your positive personal growth is important. You want to grow in the direction of your dreams so that one day the two of you meet.

There are five phases of growth success, and each of these need to become your top priority as you forge ahead and become your more authentic self. To this day, I am still working in each of these areas, so they are ongoing "works in progress." Think of them as practices that will prepare you for a better life—the one that you have deserved all along.

How to Convert Your Dreams to Reality

Some dreams[86] come and go, while others stay in your mind forever. The evergreen dreams are the ones that are toughest to realize. They often require a delicate combination of personal change and growth combined with hard work, determination, and excellent decision-making. Even then you might only get a version of your true dream.

I experienced this when I started to earn good money for the first time. It was liberating and exhilarating, and I could finally build a life for myself that I was proud of. This success brought on risks too. I ran the risk of becoming complacent, stopping myself, and turning on the cruise control. I could have forgotten about my lofty goals of starting my own business and securing ways to help my family in the future so that I could enjoy a taste of the good life.

I realized then that the only way I would ever be able to convert my dreams into reality was to maintain momentum. I had to keep going despite my successes as well as despite my failures. I think that working around success is much harder to do. Dream conversion takes such dedicated planning that you just do not expect success to derail you, but it can.

That is when I learned that momentum was non-negotiable. Sure, I would have my days off and my holidays too. My regular working days were all dedicated to my goals. I worked on each of them every day, little by little. I have never abandoned a goal that I have set for myself. By doing this, I reached a point where I had achieved them.

---

86   Adam Hill, Stop Abandoning Your Goals! 4 Ways to Turn Dreams Into Reality, http://www.mindbodygreen.com/0-10876/stop-abandoning-your-goals-4-ways-to-turn-dreams-into-reality.html

The Trick With Writing Things Down

To keep momentum going, you need to consistently practice the five phases of personal growth. The first of these involves writing things down. This sounds simple enough, yet this is a mystical and magical process that brings ideas to life. Before you write something down, it is just an idea floating in your mind; it has no legs to stand on.

Once you put it down on paper, your ideas can begin to run, jump, and leap out of you. Writing things down literally clears your mind for higher-level thinking. You naturally begin to work on what you have written down, evolving it and shaping it into a plan. You can draw it out and bring it to life in a picture, chart, or map. In other words, writing something down is an excellent way to declare that you are working on it.

When your idea moves into "working" status, you will add to it, play with it, and eventually set it in motion. Those idea legs will charge ahead and become full blown plans of action. That is the trick with writing things down. You cannot act on an idea until it is fully developed. You cannot fully develop an idea until it is written down. Those are the rules.

Plus when you write things down,[87] it helps you to process your emotions about it, and all inner conflict is dealt with. If you do not like something, you can change it. The written word then acts as a record of the past, which is a nice way of saying an "experience record." As you know, your experiences are valuable, especially since they are continually evolving.

Because of this new record, you can remember different parts of a larger plan, break it down, and reassemble it into several plans if you have to. By writing it down, you make even the largest, most complex plan completely doable. Writing helps you

---

87   Hannah Braime, How Writing Things Down Can Change Your Life, http://www. lifehack.org/articles/lifestyle/how-writing-things-down-can-change-your-life.html

think bigger, and it gives you that sense of achievement, like you have taken action on your thoughts.

Writing things down is also a secret commitment to getting them done. Your mind will flick back to that plan, and it will become a concern of yours. This is how all great plans begin. You can consciously create them by making sure that you write down any and all ideas that come to mind. Personal growth is heavily reliant on your ability to write and plan.

Write down three ideas that would help you towards a goal. Record them here:

1. _____

_____

2. _____

_____

3. _____

_____

Work on Principles of Three

Have you ever heard of the "rule of three"? It involves an efficient way to communicate ideas to yourself and to others using a simple method in writing or speaking. Concepts or ideas that are presented in threes are more interesting, enjoyable, and memorable. In other words, they stand out and facilitate understanding for everyone involved.

How can this principle[88] of the rule of three help you on your personal growth journey? This is the second phase of growth success.

---

88   Lisa B. Marshall, How to Communicate Better Using the Rule of Three, http://www.quickanddirtytips.com/business-career/public-speaking/how-to-communicate-better-using-the-rule-of-three

Throughout your writing and networking, you will find opportunities to use the rule of three to communicate more efficiently. There is something about the rhythm and pattern of these statements that make them have high impact wherever they are used.

You might use them to inspire yourself, to develop a plan, to study for a test, or to prepare a speech for your latest work presentation. I have found this simple technique invaluable as I have applied it throughout my personal growth regimen. It goes hand in hand with the two most important elements of personal growth: writing and working with people.

The rule of three had many fans in the business world, including Thomas Jefferson[89] and Steve Jobs. Jobs used the rule extensively in his communications plans, strategies, and presentations. This proves that if you want to communicate something that people will remember, use the rule of three.

This technique extends to principles as well. On any given day, only focus on three areas of your career development, or you might be spreading yourself too thin. To be the most productive, focus on your top three tasks for a day; once you are done, you will feel relieved, and everything else is a bonus! When you are going to study, split your workload into portions of three. I have found this technique to be excellent when working through large volumes of content. It works!

Whether you are creating strategies, writing, or speaking to people, this phase of your personal development can accelerate your results. My advice would be to get in the habit of using it where and when you can. It will help keep that desired momentum going by converting information into memorable experiences.

Remember, you do not have to use this all the time, only where it will have a fundamental impact. Couple it with writing most often for best results.

---

89 Carmine Gallo, Thomas Jefferson, Steve Jobs, and the Rule of 3, http://www.forbes.com/sites/carminegallo/2012/07/02/thomas-jefferson-steve-jobs-and-the-rule-of-3/

Where could you apply the rule of three in your life? Record them here:

1. _____

_____

2. _____

_____

3. _____

_____

Set Ambitions to Smart Goals

The third phase of maintaining the momentum required for long-term personal growth is to set your ambitions to smart goals. You will have short-term goals and long-term ambitions, and these will require specific smart goal structures that will need to be followed. If you have never heard of the term, a SMART goal means the following:

S – Specific
M – Measurable
A – Attainable
R – Relevant
T – Time bound

It is a mnemonic that helps you structure the way you create or build goals. Long-term ambitions will be the toughest to set as these will require detail, short-term goal planning, revamps, and updates along the way.

A SMART goal is not "I want financial security," because this contains no detail; it can never be achieved. A SMART goal is "I want to have $200,000 in my bank account by July 5, 2020." Because you have added in features that are specific, measurable, attainable, relevant, and time bound, the goal suddenly becomes achievable.

From your overall ambition[90] statement, you can work backwards and create short-term goals. It is five years to 2020, which means that you will need to put away $40,000 a year or come up with plans to generate that amount of money if this is your ultimate goal. On a smaller level, that means each month you need $3,350, or $108 a day.

While $200,000 may seem insurmountable, $108.00 is an achievable goal. You only need to break your goals down enough in order to figure out how to make them work. Then you can set your ambitions in motion, whatever they may be. Lifetime goals may include career, financial, education, family, artistic, physical, public service, or community goals.

Goal setting is a skill[91] that you need to develop at the third phase of your personal development process. I constantly revisit my goals to adjust them and set new goals all the time. It keeps the momentum going and ensures that I am achieving things each week and inching towards my ultimate dream.

When all is said and done, the only thing that matters is how quickly and efficiently you can achieve your dreams. Personal growth exists for that reason, and SMART goals ensure that you stay on the right track and on the right train moving towards your destination.

---

90 Creating a Strategy to Achieve Smart Goals, https://www.webucator.com/tutorial/goal-setting-time-management/creating-strategy-achieve-smart-goals.cfm
91 Personal Goal Setting, http://www.mindtools.com/page6.html

Speaking Truth Into Your Life

You lie to yourself all the time—did you know that? You also lie to other people all the time. Do not believe me? The last time someone asked you how you were, what did you say? Was it the truth? Exactly. "I'm fine" is almost never the truth. In the United States, we are programmed from a young age to not speak truth into our lives, and this has negative consequences.

For one, you do not recognize when you are lying to yourself—and this is a real problem when you are working on personal growth. The truth is that you are not happy with the ways things are. You are not satisfied, and it is not good enough. Why is this so hard to admit? Nothing is fine, and you know that.

From today, the denial of your feelings stops. You do not have to hide who you are anymore to compensate for other people's personal comfort. You must learn to put yourself, your life, and your feelings first. This is the ultimate truth. And you have to speak this truth into your life, or it will not manifest.

The fourth phase[92] of maintaining the momentum of your personal development is to speak truth into your life. That means being honest, at least with yourself, about who you are, how you feel, and where you want to go or what you want to do in this life. If you cannot be honest about that, then you will never reach that destination.

Speaking truth into your life means that you will be listening to yourself from now on. When you feel unhappy, you will care about yourself enough to stop and cheer yourself up. When you are sick, you will take time to recover. You are the most important person in your life because you are the one who has to get you to your end destination.

---

92 Stephenie Zamora, Why Speaking Your Truth Isn't Enough, http://www.huffingtonpost.com/stephenie-zamora/truth-_b_4640529.html

---

What do you truly want out of this life? Record it here:

_____

_____

_____

_____

_____

_____

Honoring your own truth is hard. It means saying no to friends, even if something is really important to them, because you have to tend to your own needs. It means quitting your job, moving across the country, or going back to school. It means change! Start to speak truth into your life, and amazing things will start to happen.

As an added bonus, you will experience the liberating feeling of authentic happiness for what may be the first time. Be honest with yourself, and stop living all these lies. Be who you are!

Sharing This Truth With Others

How many of your close friends and family really know who you are or what you want out of this life? I bet that it is not many. You have clutched these things close to your heart, desperate to keep them safe from the world. Unfortunately, by doing this, you have also suppressed a huge part of yourself. You have denied who you really are.

Worse yet, you have settled for a life that is making you unhappy. You do not have to do that! Society tells you lies. You can make anything you want happen if you know how. I am positive that after reading my book, you will have the tools that will get you there. That is why the fifth phase of gaining momentum with your personal development is sharing.

You need to share your internal truth with other people. Tell your family that it is your dream to live abroad. Tell your best friend that all you want to do in life is become a professional dancer. Whatever your dream, you can make it happen. But it is never going to happen if you keep denying it to yourself and to your loved ones (a side effect of harmful guilt).

When you begin to share your authentic[93] self with people, this will inspire them to set out on a journey of their own. I know because I have seen it happen many times. Just by sharing my story of struggle, survival, and success, I have helped many people already. There will be a lot of unrealized dreams being pursued because of me. I am happy about that, and I hope that it continues with you.

So if you are serious about maintaining personal growth and development—so that you can one day deserve the dreams that you have—it is time to tell everyone you know what it is you want: that main goal that keeps you up at night, the one that would set you free. It does not matter if it is big as long as it is realistic.

Speaking the truth is not enough, it is true—you have to live it. I have given you the tools you need to run screaming towards success; now you need to let go of the lies that you have been living in and tell the world. If you want to live a life of passion, authenticity, and fulfillment, then you will take this truth-telling phase very seriously.

---

93   Mike Robbins, Speak Your Truth, http://www.oprah.com/spirit/Speak-Your-Truth_2

What is that one single goal that you must achieve in life? Record it here:

What five phases do you need to keep the momentum going for personal growth?

Outline five actions that you need to take to move forward with personal growth:

_____

_____

_____

_____

_____

_____

EXCELLENCE: HOW DO YOU INSPIRE OTHERS?

CHAPTER 13

Becoming the Mentor Motivator

"Excellence is an art won by training and habituation. We do not act rightly because we have virtue or excellence, but we rather have those because we have acted rightly. We are what we repeatedly do. Excellence, then, is not an act but a habit."

Aristotle

Once you have worked hard for several years and have drawn closer to your goals, there is a point where your life begins to rapidly improve. This is the point where it is your duty to share your excellence and how it was acquired with other people. Inspiring others is not a selfless act; it is actually something you need to do to continue moving forward—sharing and passing it on to others.

You have reached the final section in the WEDGE system—"E" for excellence. Understanding yourself and who you are leads to one inevitable thing—being able to help others. This is a main goal for many people because it inspires you to greater heights. The ability to help others succeed is a gift that will take you far beyond anything you could imagine.

My Life, My Vision: The Tipping Point

I faced a choice—stay in my comfortable job or take another risk to follow another dream. A few months passed, and I was connected with a director leading a team of engineers and project managers in Miami, FL. The director was looking for someone with a background in both, and something told me that I had to go for it. She was a Latina leader with a background in engineering and psychology, so it was a goldmine mentoring opportunity.

I had several subsequent interviews with her, including one with the Senior Industrial Engineer and various directors in the organization. It was almost Independence Day in 2014 when I got the call with the offer. The very next day I was also extended an amazing opportunity with my former COO, this time in a project manager role in Connecticut—another crossroads and bigger questions.

Do I move down to Miami and chase my dreams with the new company that I had not even visited, or do I move one state south with a reliable mentor I know and trust? I had one day to make my decision, and it was an intense 24-hour period of self-reflection. I chose my dream and accepted the Engineering/Project Management position in Miami. I was given three weeks to pick up my life and get there, which was an aggressive deadline to say the least, but I knew I had to make it work.

Even once you have achieved your dream, you need to keep building on it. Again, Mami's voice rang in my mind: "You can do anything you put your mind to," and I still believe that. Doors will wedge open up just a sliver; then you have to burst through them. Today, my director, mentors, and new team are teaching me strategy and organizational development. Next stop, top tier management!

Encouraged by one of my mentors, I finally formalized the creation of my own business dedicated to transforming others and empowering them with the tools to become the best versions of themselves. That is my ultimate purpose—to inspire others to take action and remind them that they are in control.

Do you remember the puppy in my dreams too? I had my mind on him for years, and I finally got my puppy (named Buzz Lightyear) just in time before the New Year in 2015 as well!

Why Inspiration Is a Powerful Tool

I believe that my secret to success has been my ability to help other people along the way. The ability to inspire others and lift them along with you is something that can and will take you higher than you can go alone. Beyond your goals and your job description, there will always be people. They are a fundamental element in your life.

At the end of it all, you are not going to look back and think, "All that lovely money I spent…it was so worth it." You are going to think about all the people whose lives you touched. You can start doing that already so that by the time you rise up, it is a good habit of yours. Anyone can work and do well, but legends are made by inspiring others.

So it is a two-way street. The more people you help, the more people will want to help you. As you help others, they will lift you up. In order to inspire people, you need to be authentic and living the life you were meant to live no matter what. People respect that and want to know how they can also get to that point.

Inspiration[94] is a powerful tool because it makes you a leader, a motivator, a mentor, and a teacher. Anyone can be a leader in any context, and they can do better in their careers because they foster a sense of trust, credibility, and reliability, which many asset-minded people do not have. As a tool, it can be used to take you to the best places in the world.

---

94 Andrew Olson, Why Inspiring Others Is the Secret to Success, http://blog. brazencareerist.com/2012/03/27/why-inspiring-others-is-the-secret-to-success/

People want someone to lead them to a better place, and you can be that inspirational leader once you have crossed the threshold. Start as a mentor, and work your way up to inspirational leader. By inspiring people, you can help them progress towards their goals, which is very fulfilling—all while progressing toward your own goals.

Harvard[95] calls inspiration the "springboard for creativity," and it can improve everything from being innovative, to writing, creating, building, and designing. You need to be the example that instills inspiration in other people. It is infectious if you get it right. I believe that if enough "at-risk" youth inspire each other, the categorization will disappear altogether.

Use this powerful tool to communicate with others in a meaningful way that positively impacts their lives. They will never forget you, and you will become a happier person for it. There is no feeling like helping others improve their own lives. If you get a chance to do it, my advice would be to do it.

Creating Good Karma: The Rules

I am a firm believer in good karma. I believe that if you actively do good things and help others, good things will step into your life. I have found this to be very true, so I thought I would share some rules about creating good karma in your own lives. Pay attention to these rules; they are endorsed by the Dalai Lama[96] himself!

- The first rule of good karma is to take into account that great love and great achievements involve great risk. You cannot have one without the other.

---

95 Scott Barry Kaufman, Why Inspiration Matters, https://hbr.org/2011/11/why-inspiration-matters/

96 The Dalai Lama, 20 Ways to Get Good Karma, http://www.spiritualnow.com/articles/25/1/20-Ways-to-Get-Good-Karma/Page1.html

---

How would you inspire someone? Record it here:

_____

_____

_____

_____

_____

_____

- You should strive to follow the three "R"s—respect yourself, respect others, and take responsibility for all of your actions.
- Never forget that not getting what you want sometimes is a wonderful stroke of luck.
- Once you have realized that you have made a mistake, immediately seek to correct it. Accepting fault is a strength and should be seen that way.
- Always open your arms to change, but do not let go of your values. Live a good, honorable life. When you get older and think back, you will be able to enjoy it a second time.
- In disagreements with loved ones, deal only with the current situation. Leave the past in the past, where it belongs.
- Judge your success by what you had to give up in order to get it.
- If you want others to be happy, practice compassion. If you want to be happy yourself, practice compassion.
- The best kind of relationship is the one in which your love for each other exceeds your need for each other.

- Believe in the law of cause[97] and effect; it is working in your life. What you sow, so shall you reap. If you want happiness, be happy. If you want peace, be peaceful. These are the actions you must take to be who you want to be.

- You are part of creation and a creator. That is why you create your own existence. Be yourself, and surround yourself with what you want to have in your present day life. This will make you happy, and that is the goal of life.

- In order to grow, you must go. Change is the catalyst that causes growth, not the people, places, and things around us. All you have is yourself; learn to change what is in your heart to move towards better things.

These incredible karmic rules are in play in your life. Make sure that you consider them before you take action, and work them into your life strategies and plans.

Seizing Opportunities to Inspire Change

Inspiring change in others is perhaps the highest calling of all. This is because change is the catalyst that helps people grow, and with every moment of inspiration, they inch closer towards who they really are and what they want out of life.

As a mentor and leader, you need to focus on the opportunities[98] that will arise in your own life where you can inspire the most change. Because of society and the many systems that we face, there are usually only two routes—to be part of the problem or to be part of the solution. I want to encourage you to seize opportunities to help others when they present themselves.

---

97   E.C. LaMeaux, How to Attract Good Karma, http://life.gaiam.com/article/how-attract-good-karma

98   Daniel Wallen, The Simplest Ways to Inspire People and Change Their Life, http://www.lifehack.org/articles/communication/20-ways-inspire-people-around-you.html

- Become a mentor and inspire[99] someone else, or several other people, to step up in life and pursue their dreams. No one is a threat to you or your job. You are on your own path. Educating and helping someone else is the fastest route to success and will help you learn new things. Invest in the happiness of others!

- Step into a leadership role. If you see other people floundering, be bold, and step in to help them (if you are wanted). Connect emotionally with these people, and then guide them towards what they should be doing instead of what they are doing. Everyone needs a role model and a leader. You can be that person for someone else.

- Innovation is the product of inspiration, so spread it where you can—in your team environments, in student groups, and at meetings. Propose new ways to do things, and get people thinking creatively. Be the change you want to see wherever you are.

- Change comes from action; you need to be the leader inspiring that action. Help people understand why things need to change for the better and evolve into something new. Stagnancy only breeds more of the same.

When you seize opportunities to inspire change, you will find that doors start to crack open all around you. This is the WEDGE Effect hard at work. The more opportunities you can create for others, the more that will open for you. Then it is up to you to pick a door and burst through it. With your dreams at the helm, there will be nothing stopping you from getting there.

Inspiring people can be as small as caring about someone's bad day. It can be as large as being enthusiastic in front of a team of people that have just suffered a defeat. You need to earn the

---

99   3 Ideas to Inspire Change, http://georgecouros.ca/blog/archives/3842

trust of those around you to make things happen. Another big component of inspiring change in others is sticking with your positive attitude.

People will want to see you living what you preach before they can accept what you say to them. Be strong, be bold, and focus on building people up instead of tearing them down.

Where do you see opportunities to inspire change in your life? Record them here:

_____

_____

_____

_____

_____

Impacting the Lives of Others

There is a method to impacting the lives of others that I want you to consider before you strike out into the world and gets things done. First of all, you cannot help anyone before you help yourself. Sacrificing your physical, emotional, and mental states to help others does not help them, and it certainly does not help you.

Real impact comes when you can stand as an example to others and help them enough to effect real change. You could spend years making healthy recipes for people looking to eat healthier, but if you do not know how to teach them how to do it themselves, they will never stop asking you for the food. Real impact means real change.

How could you impact the lives of others?
Record it here:

_____

_____

_____

_____

_____

_____

Once you have sorted out your own life[100] and become a real inspiration to those around you, then you can begin to help them. Do not bother to counsel others before you have been counseled. Do not run before you can walk. There is a natural order to things, and even if you are a quick learner, you also need to experience the trials of setting things right.

If you do not go through the entire WEDGE Effect process first, then you will only be halfway through that door when the people in your life start taking your time. Without experience, you could end up being diverted off your path, and that means trouble. Never allow the work you do for others to affect the goals that you want to reach for yourself.

The goal is to improve your life, not perfect it. Leave lots of room for mistakes on both sides. You will make mistakes, and the people you try to help will make mistakes. This is not the end of the world; you can always start again. Changing the world takes a lot of false starts, but as long as your heart is changed first, it is possible.

100 Kathy Caprino, 9 Core Behaviors of People Who Positively Impact the World, http://www.forbes.com/sites/kathycaprino/2014/06/02/9-core-behaviors-of-people-who-positively-impact-the-world/

Right now look for little ways that you can positively impact the lives of others. Over time, as you move through the ranks, increase your efforts and devote more time to helping others for more impact. Once you are in a leadership position, it is easy to become selfish and ignore your community or the people that need a moment of support. Do not be that person!

Real success is always built through networks of people. They raise you up or pull you down depending on who you are and how you have helped them. Remember to always have a positive and gracious attitude throughout this process, and stay humble. There is a fine line between helping and preaching.

The Lives I've Influenced (Interview Spotlight)

As part of my interview process, I asked some fellow mentors why mentoring is important and what the most valuable lessons were that it taught them. Here you will see the unedited answers from the people in my life.

Claudine Johnson: Where my mother was unable to help me, that is where mentors, like those who I worked with at Bottom Line and Posse, were able to fill the gap. They spoke with me about getting through college, financial aid, job search, building my brand, how to carry myself in certain environments, and so much more. For students, especially those who come from low income and underrepresented backgrounds, it is important to have mentors that they can depend on. One of the most important lessons I learned was that I was brought into the world for a purpose. To always be my authentic self, to never change who I am to fit in, and to remember that the work I do is not for man but for God.

Dan Prestegaard: Mentoring is important because it changes lives. It encourages growth and improvement and has a broad contribution to society. I learned to play the long game—just like investments, experiences and lessons compound. What you learn and do early in life carries forward and has a multiplier effect on benefits. If I learn something today, it not only helps me with today, it makes me aware of more possibilities and helps me see and do more tomorrow and into the future.

Lissety Keon: Based on my own personal experience, mentoring has been mostly informal. It has come from many angles and people at all levels. I have never sought to have a formal mentorship but instead I have fostered relationships where I see integrity, professional expertise, and a positive attitude. As we grow in our professional and personal lives, we need role models or mentors to help us navigate the multiple bumps we will find on our way. To help us get up, to show us that life means much more than the issue at hand, and above all, to be true proof that we deserve all the good that happens to us. There are two lessons that have helped me transition to the person I am today. Number one: your life and happiness are much more than your success. Number two: once all your needs are satisfied, what is an individual left with? The desire to leave a legacy, make an impact, help others. These two conversations continue to bring me to self-reflection and mindfulness.

Omar Otero: It's the opportunity for the person (mentor) to give back. By not taking this opportunity, the potential mentor then loses a chance to grow as an individual. The law of reciprocity allows the mentor to learn more about him or herself while teaching others. Mentoring is more important for the mentor than the mentee.

How do you see yourself inspiring others in the future?

_____

_____

_____

_____

_____

_____

Name five areas where you could have the most impact on other people:

1. _____

_____

2. _____

_____

3. _____

_____

4. _____

_____

5. _____

_____

CHAPTER 14

The Equality of Excellent

"Dreams can become a reality when we possess a vision that is characterized by the willingness to work hard, a desire for excellence, and a belief in our right and our responsibility to be equal members of society."
Janet Jackson

Excellence can mean getting to the top of your field, or it can mean reaching your personal goal. No one can really define it but you. Everyone has that little voice inside that knows when you would have tried hard enough to succeed. At that moment, you would have achieved excellence—not in what you now have but in what you have already done.

Being the best often comes with a new set of problems and responsibilities, which is why growth never stops. There are always new goals and greater heights to reach. When you do finally reach that threshold, it is up to you to pass on the knowledge that got you there. If we all had to do this, our communities would be that much stronger.

How Being the Best Drives the Wedge Open

Excellence by its very definition is something that goes beyond the norm. You will have to learn how to live a life of excellence if you are going to achieve and then surpass your goals. One of the most important things that will get you there is striking that ideal balance.

You have to learn to be mindful of yourself while focusing on what is meaningful and important in your life. Plus you need to find time to reach out and help others. Your happiness will happen naturally on this journey as your mind, body, and spirit become united in purpose and intent.

When this happens, you are at your best, and nothing can stop you from converting every opportunity into something positive for yourself and the people that you care about. Ultimately, once you reach your dream, you realize that the whole time it was not the dream that mattered but the process of becoming the kind of person who deserves that dream.

Being the best drives the wedge of opportunity open because of what you have learned and who you have become. These skills, built from trial and error, failure and struggle, will be the things that make you intrinsically successful for the rest of your life. This is the investment you make in yourself when you practice the WEDGE Effect.

Actively Pursuing Excellence

When you actively pursue excellence in your daily schedule, the world will open up for you. That is because excellence is an attitude and a way of conducting yourself on a daily basis. Society rewards those that pursue excellence.

Take Olympic athletes for example—they live, eat, breathe, and sleep excellence. If one element in their schedule falls out of step, it throws off their entire training program. This is how you should live—like each day is an opportunity and you have to be on your best form to make it happen. What that meant for me was:

- I adopted a healthy lifestyle and fed my body and brain high quality food. I cut out the junk because I knew that it would prevent me from being my best.

- I set routines that would keep me working and managing my time efficiently so that I would achieve my goals little by little.

- I made sure that my body got enough exercise so that I could lower my stress levels and keep in good shape despite demanding work hours.

- I focused on doing my work to the best of my ability, and when there were problems, I would "hack" my way through them.

- I made sure that I got enough sleep so that I would be refreshed each day and able to work through my intense schedules (I did not do too well with this in college, but I really started valuing this as a career woman).

- I practiced stress management techniques to keep myself on track and my anxiety in check so that I did not lose focus or derail my progress.

How do you actively pursue excellence in your life?

Excellence[101] means striving for quality and merit in everything that you do. When you live this way, you can be proud of the way that you spend your precious time. Time will take care of the rest, and soon you will be knocking at the door of your dreams.

Mental Conditioning: Your Road to Great Things

Athletes training for competitive sports go through rigorous training programs in order to be able to achieve the amazing physical and mental feats that they can. I have always considered reaching for your life goals and desired future as the biggest events in your life. Of course, you need to train for it so that you can make it all the way to the end.

And to some degree this requires mental conditioning to get right. Athletes use mental conditioning to streamline their efforts in their chosen sport. They have to be strong, fit, and resilient enough to roll with the punches on a competitive level.

Mental conditioning[102] is what keeps a long distance runner pushing through the pain to stay at a certain pace to win the race. It is what keeps a white water kayaker calm and making the right strokes when they experience turbulent water and get caught in a hole. This emulates real life, which is why mental conditioning can come in handy.

- Practice being hardline[103] with your schedule. This is the most important thing in your life because it is your path to great things. Do not blow it off because you "have time."
- Train your brain to be productive by limiting distractions all around it. Turn off your phone and your television and only

101 Salman Khan, Why Pursue Excellence, http://www.academia.edu/4091169/Why_pursue_Excellence

102 Alex Hutchinson, Cracking the Athlete's Brain, http://www.outsideonline.com/fitness/mental-conditioning/Head-Games-Brain-Injuries-Study-Athletes.html

103 Nadia Goodman, How to Stay Focused: Train Your Brain, http://www.entrepreneur.com/blog/225321

go out when you have designated break time for yourself. This is how you move through set schedules quickly.

- Deliberately allocating your time is a great method of keeping yourself in check. Schedule in time for work and time to relax. Do not deviate from it.
- Train your brain to focus on one to three important things every day outside of your normal working hours at school or at work. That way you limit your focus and do not get overwhelmed with work.

Your brain is a muscle, and the more you condition it to work consistently, the better off you will be. Like athletes that need to win the race, you can also win that long-term race of yours by practicing discipline, focus, and commitment to your goals.

How can you train your brain to stick to your schedule?

The Culture of Shared Success

Have you ever heard the phrase "iron sharpens iron"? It relates to the way that one motivated person has the ability to help another reach higher than they would if they were alone. People that are driven to succeed need to stick together so that they can create a culture of shared success in their lives.

No one in the world has ever succeeded alone; it always takes other people to guide them and help them along the way. If you can acknowledge this and actively work it into your plan and lifestyle, you will realize that you can attain success faster.

I would not be where I am today without people mentoring[104] me and taking a chance on me when I interviewed for those jobs as a fresh face back in college. I had no experience, but I was given the opportunity to prove my worth by people that believed in me.

In the same way, you need to cultivate this kind of culture in your life. The "pay it forward" culture of being helped and helping others who want to succeed keeps you in the right circles, and it gives your life goals a boost.

This sort of attitude and outlook drives success as people see you helping others and are therefore more inclined to help you. It creates a feedback loop of success that you can ride all the way to the top. This kind of culture is a very valuable tool that promotes excellence in your life and in the lives of your mentors and mentees.

Sharing your success also fosters an abundance mindset, whereas most people are stuck in the scarcity mindset. They are afraid to share what they know with other people or to genuinely help them in case they are overtaken. But this should not be a fear of yours. If a mentee overtakes you, good for them! You have different life goals.

Always promote that culture of shared success to experience the benefits of good karma and powerful long-term relationships in business. You will see just how valuable this is as you move through the WEDGE Effect.

---

104 John Morgan, Why You Should Share Your Success, http://johnmichaelmorgan. com/why-you-should-share-your-success/

Describe how you would feel if you helped someone become successful:

_____

_____

_____

_____

_____

Raising Others Higher: How to Get Ahead

If you take a close look at your goals, you will realize that once you have achieved what you set out to achieve, the end result of that is to help other people. That is why it is so important to help people throughout your process—because it gives you good training for the main event.

The best leaders[105] and mentors I have ever had taught me that helping others get ahead is the underlying point of their lives. When you can serve others and help them realize their dreams, you are adding to your value and equity as a person of excellence.

It is no wonder then that leaders who do this are often prized because they are givers. These individuals are considerate and compassionate, and they care about their employees' feelings. They want to see each individual succeed in the personal sense, and it shows.

Once I began to practice this theory, more and more doors wedged open for me. When you raise others above yourself, you

---

105 Susan Dominus, Is Giving the Secret to Getting Ahead?, http://www.nytimes.com/2013/03/31/magazine/is-giving-the-secret-to-getting-ahead.html?pagewanted=all&_r=0

get ahead a lot faster. It sounds selfish to say, but being a giver is just about the quickest route to success that I know!

Helping other people[106] is not a time-sapping energy diversion like many people perceive it to be. You are human, and you are driven to have social relationships that are rewarding. When you invest in the success of others, it motivates you, increases your own productivity and creativity, and gives you feelings of fulfillment.

Self-interest has limited benefits in the workplace, and a "give and take" attitude is much more valuable. This way you learn more, you make more social connections that can be helpful in your career, and it makes you more visible to senior management. You would be surprised how few people genuinely take the time to help. This is your wedge in!

Name three ways you can help raise someone higher in life:

1. _____

_____

2. _____

_____

3. _____

_____

---

106 Lisa Quast, To Get Ahead, Help Develop Others' Careers, http://www.forbes.com/sites/lisaquast/2012/10/01/to-get-ahead-in-your-career-develop-others/

Business Success Starts Here

When you can rapidly accelerate through your career, learning from others—guess what? You end up with a whole lot of knowledge while you are still young enough to make real use of it. That means that you can open your own business at a younger age and enjoy real success from it if you want to.

I believe that business success starts with a heart for giving. When you have nurtured the attitude that anyone that wants help can get it, you naturally become a leader. Not only does mentoring teach you how to lead but it also shows you how to manage and work with people.

Gaining success[107] in business uses the same models as gaining success in life. You need to constantly educate yourself and stay orientated in your field. Surrounding yourself with like-minded people will cause that "iron on iron" effect, where you can all learn from each other and create a culture of sharing and excellence.

This makes for a very sound business foundation, and you can build great things here. With great success comes great responsibility, I like to say. You can never take your success for granted. Even though you worked hard to achieve it, you absorbed knowledge from others, and you need to give that back.

There are people in the world who want to succeed; they just need the opportunity. When you run your own business, you can put them in positions where they can prove themselves to you. By mentoring them, you are helping your own company succeed, and you are investing in the personal equity of someone else's success.

For the most part, this aligns with all the laws of good karma, and great things will happen in your company. If you do not believe me, try it out. I dare you to use the WEDGE Effect in

---

107 Eddie Cuffin, The 10 Ways to Achieve Success in Both Business and Life, http://elitedaily.com/money/entrepreneurship/10-ways-to-be-successful-in-business-and-in-life/

business and not have a positive outcome. When you are there for people, they are there for you—and any business leader will tell you this is how successful companies are built.

How would you help the people around you thrive?

_____

_____

_____

_____

_____

_____

Bullet point ways of helping others at work:

_____

_____

_____

_____

_____

_____

CHAPTER 15

A Mind for Mentoring

"Mentors provide professional networks, outlets for frustration, college and career counseling, general life advice, and most importantly, an extra voice telling a student they are smart enough and capable enough to cross the stage at graduation and land their first paycheck from a career pathway job."
Gerald Chertavian

The last phase of your journey should be concerned with developing your mentoring mind. As I have mentioned, these mentor relationships are very valuable, and they teach you a lot about yourself. When you take on the responsibility of mentoring someone, their success becomes paramount to yours.

There are many other benefits to mentoring that remain unseen until you become a mentor yourself. Then you finally realize why all of your mentors worked so hard to help you. Along with the satisfaction and fulfillment you get for helping people, you also realize that you have built a personal culture of growth for yourself that keeps you moving forward.

Choosing Your Social Group

I did not regret a second of moving to Miami to pursue my dream job. It led me to establishing my own business and starting my work to create a non-profit so that I could focus more on helping those around me that had faced similar challenges to me.

At every stage in your growth, friends will come and go. Your social group, however, helps determine where you go and how far you get to reach. Choosing your social group can be difficult, and mentoring makes it easier. When you are interested in helping and guiding others, you will never be short of like-minded people.

This in turn creates a personal culture of growth and development that will take you places. You will never have friends that hold you back or dislike your success. Because of mentoring and being mentored, you will be exposed to both sides of the social spectrum meeting up and down the ladder to remain orientated in what you want for your future.

How have the friends in your past impacted your success? Remember, people can only be positive or negative influences.

Expecting Excellence: What to Do

One of my mentors once told me, "Do not expect perfection; expect excellence," and this has stuck with me through the years. To become the kind of person who is consciously pursuing excellence,[108] you need to center yourself in some daily practices:

- *You are what you think about.* What you are thinking about today will impact how you perform. If you wake up in a bad mood or feel anxious, have a protocol in place to bring your mood back from that. Rein in those negative thoughts, exercise, or practice affirmations until you feel ready for your day.

- *Do not forget to simplify things.* Life can get complicated and crowded. If you need to take time for yourself, do it. Do not listen to what other people say; they will still be there tomorrow. For today, if you need to simplify things, do it for your own sanity.

- *How you are with people is who you are.* You can learn more about yourself through the interactions that you have with others. If you spot insecurity, hostility, or any other negative traits, start working on them. Anything can be reprogrammed if it goes onto your agenda. Add it to your life plan, and set some goals.

- *Stop taking sides.* It is human nature to divide things into right and wrong, good and bad, but these are just methods of understanding complex ideas. Do not confuse how you feel or what you think with who you are. Remain neutral and thrive! There are no rules against not picking sides.

- *You do not need validation or to be dependent on another person.* You exist to live up to your own expectations of yourself, not to someone else's expectations. Your ego might confuse this with other things, but ultimately you decide how to feel.

---

108 The 8 Keys of Excellence – Definitions and Descriptions, http://www.8keys. org/8keys_defined.aspx

- *Always expect excellence from your mentees, but give them room to make mistakes.* How you make them feel will either set them on the path or force them off it.

Being a proactive person[109] with a positive attitude and a heart of gratitude is enough to reach for excellence in all things. Set goals, both realistic and unrealistic ones, and challenge yourself. You never know what you can achieve when you work on it all the time.

How are you proactively inspiring excellence in your life each day?

Teaching Through Personal Growth

One of the final and most poignant methods of growing is to teach others. You may remember in many of the learning styles we mentioned earlier that teaching often came up as a way to remember, remind, and inspire yourself as well as your students.

Because personal growth is an ongoing concern, having these mentor relationships keeps you searching for growth of your own. You will see issues in other people that reside in yourself. You will learn from them, exchange ideas, and grow into better people together.

---

109 Mary Jo Asmus, Expect Excellence, http://smartblogs.com/leadership/2014/02/05/expect-excellence/

The best teachers are the ones that educate their mentees based on personal experience. As a Latina who comes from an "at-risk" background, I always felt like my journey to where I am now could be used to inspire others and help them realize their own potential.

When you focus on personal growth,[110] you cannot keep it to yourself. It just does not work like that. Instead, you need to share it with others so that they can grow too. Then you need to teach them to "pay it forward." With enough work and luck, hopefully more lives will change.

Never forget that paths are made by walking. Experience cannot be taught, but it can be communicated. Mentoring accelerates learning and gets people to where they need to be in life faster, which makes the potential for helping others greater. Doing good deeds for other people or paying it forward has become my personal life philosophy.

Imagine you are all flowers in a garden. Each of you is growing according to your own speed and in your own time. There is plenty of sun, water, and nutrients for everyone. The only thing that is missing is in which direction to grow. Smaller flowers reach up; larger flowers bend down. That is how it works in nature.

What kind of impact would success have on your friends and family? Share the knowledge!

_____

_____

_____

---

110 Viral Mehta, Servant Leadership: Helping People Come Alive, https://www.psychologytoday.com/blog/pay-it-forward/201207/servant-leadership-helping-people-come-alive

Creativity and the Mentoring Mind

When you have a mind for mentoring, you will fall in love with the act of passing down knowledge. When you learn something new and find it to be true, you will feel compelled to share this message with everyone that you know.

By its very nature, mentoring inspires creativity. I would say that the act of mentoring generates creativity in both parties. When you share and exchange insight with others, your creative juices begin to flow. Then you become inspired with your own work.

At the same time, your mentee will become inspired and creative, and they will go out into the world and communicate, sharing ideas and improving their own lives in creative ways. Encouraging and motivating others is a creative process in itself. Once you learn how to do it, it is a skill that will never stop giving back to you.

That is why I want to challenge you to take on mentees of your own as soon as you feel ready. I have used the creativity inspired by my mentor–mentee relationships to fuel my life goals and drive for many years. These social connections and the positive experiences that result from them are fuel for your internal fire.

When I became a mentor, I realized how gratifying it was to help another person. I needed this kind of investment to validate my efforts and propel myself forward. That is why mentor–mentee relationships are a give and take. It is not just the mentor dumping information on the mentee; at every step, there is a creative exchange that benefits both parties.

A mentoring partnership[111] is an enriching experience both socially and creatively; it allows you to develop your own communication and leadership skills while you help someone else build a better life for themselves. Having a "mentoring mind" is a big skill that leaders look for in up and coming talent today, so it helps to know how.

111 Mentoring, http://www.mindtools.com/pages/article/newCDV_70.htm

> **Share the WEDGE Effect with a friend. Do you feel more creative?**
>
> _____
>
> _____
>
> _____
>
> _____

Confidence and Challenging Convention

To live the life that you have always wanted is going to require confidence, and that means a lot of trial and error so that you can be sure that you are doing, and have done, the right thing. Confidence[112] comes from doing; it does not come from thinking.

You might not believe that you can achieve your life goal right now, but that is because you lack confidence. Nothing in your life has said, "Hey, this is possible" until now. Being unsure of yourself is a poison. It makes you afraid to start along a new path and try new things. This limits your potential and minimizes your ability to impact the world around you.

The first step for you will be to challenge those limiting beliefs that have held you down all this time. You formed those opinions years ago, but it is time that they change. The way to change them is to gradually build up your confidence as you challenge convention in your life. This means working through some small steps as well as some big changes.

112 Lori Deschene, 8 Ways to Be More Confident: Live the Life of Your Dreams, http://tinybuddha.com/blog/8-ways-to-be-more-confident-live-the-life-of-your-dreams/

- *Become more self-aware.* Understand why you are afraid and how it has impacted your life so far.
- *Understand your strengths and weaknesses, and know that learning who you are is an ongoing pursuit.* Figure out who you want to be, and realize the confidence that it will take you to get there.
- *Expect success.* When you start at something, do not quit until you succeed. If you do not succeed, find out why. Get help from other people. Build your confidence in areas where you are weak.
- *Trust your capabilities, and seize opportunities.* Even when someone criticizes you, see it as an opportunity for growth. Never allow anyone to strip you of your confidence; you will need it to succeed.

Confidence helps you challenge what you know, which is essential in bridging knowledge gaps. Do not forget to work on yours, and help you mentees work on theirs. Together you can grow into highly confident people.

Becoming the Success You Aimed For

Success is a very personal thing. Only you can decide when you achieve it and when your inner self will be appeased by what you have done. Even then, you cannot stop. A person that achieves success needs to keep going, keep sharing, and keep evolving.

Success is just the beginning of your life's journey. To become the success that you aim for, you need to follow the WEDGE Effect very carefully, and it will take you all the way. At this point you have the information that you need to thrive, but this still needs to be transformed into knowledge. That can only be done via practice and experience.

- Create the WISHES that you have for yourself in this life.

- EDUCATE yourself so that you are prepared to take them on.
- Focus on maintaining your DRIVE so that you never stop moving forward.
- GROW into your dreams by becoming deserving of them.
- Foster an attitude of EXCELLENCE, and pay it forward.

With the WEDGE Effect, you can take yourself from the life that you have now to the life that you know you deserve. Listen to that voice inside you, the one that says, "There must be something more for me," and take a step towards your own happiness.

No one in the world but you can make this happen. Your success belongs to you and you alone. To evolve into this person, you have to concede that a lot of hard work is ahead of you. You will have to focus for a long time to get what you want out of life.

But the good news is that this journey will be the most rewarding you have ever experienced. You will learn who you are and what you want out of life. You will make new friends and experience new things. Above all, you will become who you were meant to be.

Describe how the WEDGE Effect will get you to success:

_____

_____

_____

_____

_____

_____

_____

_____

_____

_____

Create a bullet point list of what you should do next:

_____

_____

_____

_____

_____

_____

CONCLUSION

You have reached the end of the WEDGE Effect, and now you understand how to move forward to pursue your life goals and become the best version of yourself. Success is waiting for you. It has been waiting for you all along.

All you need to do now is close this book and take that first step along your path. You do not have to accept that you are going to struggle with poverty for the rest of your life. Like me, you can reject your label as an "at-risk" youth.

The only risk you face now is what will happen if you ignore this opportunity. The WEDGE Effect was not designed to give you all of the answers. It was designed to show you how to find all of the answers.

There is something inside you that wants to be released. This potential wants to bloom into something incredible in this world. But you have to nurture it first. You have to find out where to plant your roots, how much sun you need, and when you need to be watered.

Do not give up on yourself! The only thing that stands between you and success is a lack of knowledge. Do what you must to improve your life and the lives of others. Together we can make sure that every "at-risk" child has a real shot at success.

Join me by becoming a graduate of the WEDGE Effect. Life has many closed doors, but we only need a little, tiny wedge to burst through. Once you begin, you will see wedges everywhere. Then it is just a matter of picking the right one and running for your life.

Do not be afraid to take action, even if it is just writing down a plan. Remember, the key to success is to begin and to not end until you get there.

To your success!
Iris J. González

REFERENCES

Chapter 1

Success Quotes – Page 2, http://www.brainyquote.com/quotes/topics/topic_success2.html

Key Concepts: Brain Architecture, http://developingchild.harvard.edu/key_concepts/brain_architecture/

Key Concepts: Toxic Stress, http://developingchild.harvard.edu/key_concepts/toxic_stress_response/

Gerwin, Carol, *Tackling Toxic Stress, Pediatricians Take On Toxic Stress,* http://developingchild.harvard.edu/resources/stories_from_the_field/tackling_toxic_stress/pediatricians_take_on_toxic_stress/

Key Concepts: Executive Function, http://developingchild.harvard.edu/key_concepts/executive_function/

The Effects Of Childhood Stress In Health Across The Lifespan, http://www.cdc.gov/ncipc/pub-res/pdf/Childhood_Stress.pdf

Advancing the Self-Sufficiency And Well-Being Of At-Risk Youth: A Conceptual Framework, http://www.acf.hhs.gov/programs/opre/resource/advancing-the-self-sufficiency-and-well-being-of-at-risk-youth-a-conceptual

At-Risk Students, http://en.wikipedia.org/wiki/At-risk_students

Youth From Low Income Families, http://aspe.hhs.gov/hsp/09/vulnerableyouth/3/index.shtml

Grayson, Randall, PhD, *At-Risk Youth & Resilience Factors,* http://www.visionrealization.com/Resources/Camper_Devel/At-risk_youth_presentation.pdf

Situations That Put Youth At Risk, http://www.dropoutprevention.org/statistics/situations-that-put-youth-at-risk

Types Of Traumatic Stress, http://www.nctsnet.org/trauma-types#q2

Complex Trauma, http://www.nctsnet.org/trauma-types/complex-trauma

Effects Of Complex Trauma, http://www.nctsn.org/trauma-types/complex-trauma/effects-of-complex-trauma

Cross, Kim, *Complex Trauma In Early Childhood,* http://www.aaets.org/article174.htm

Chapter 2

Wish Quotes, http://www.brainyquote.com/quotes/keywords/wish.html

Lemind, Anna, *How To Make Your Wishes Come True By The Power Of Thought,* http://www.learning-mind.com/how-to-make-your-wishes-come-true-by-the-power-of-thought/

The Power Of Belief, http://www.fragmentsweb.org/fourtx/powbeltx.html

The Power Of Belief, http://ukcatalogue.oup.com/product/9780198530107.do

Law Of Attraction – The Power Of Beliefs, http://www.mind-sets.com/html/law_of_attraction/the_power_of_beliefs.htm

Lickerman, Alex, *The Two Kinds Of Belief,* http://www.psychologytoday.com/blog/happiness-in-world/201104/the-two-kinds-belief

How Can You Change From A Fixed Mindset To A Growth Mindset? http://mindsetonline.com/changeyourmindset/firststeps/

Scarbro, Denise, *Stop The Insanity: Get Out Of Your Head,* http://www.huffingtonpost.com/denise-scarbro/stop-negative-thoughts_b_2295084.html

Krull, Erika, *Depression And Letting Go Of Negative Thoughts,* http://psychcentral.com/lib/depression-and-letting-go-of-negative-thoughts/0003764

Chapter 3

Desire Quotes, http://www.brainyquote.com/quotes/keywords/desire.html

The Importance Of Hard Work In Success, http://www.selfgrowth.com/articles/the_importance_of_hard_work_in_success

Time Management, http://www.psychologytoday.com/basics/time-management

Hyatt, Michael, *Creating Your Personal Life Plan,* http://michaelhyatt.com/creating-your-life-plan

Britt, Kate, *How To Change Your Mind And Your Life By Using Affirmations,* http://tinybuddha.com/blog/how-to-change-your-mind-and-your-life-by-using-affirmations/

Using Affirmations – Harnessing Positive Thinking, http://www.mindtools.com/pages/article/affirmations.htm

Chapter 4

Learning Quotes, http://www.brainyquote.com/quotes/topics/topic_learning.html

Bernard, Sara, *Neuroplasticity: Learning Physically Changes The Brain,* http://www.edutopia.org/neuroscience-brain-based-learning-neuroplasticity

Willis, Judy, *The Neuroscience Of Joyful Education,* http://www.ascd.org/publications/educational-leadership/summer07/vol64/num09/The-Neuroscience-of-Joyful-Education.aspx

Active Learning, http://www.cte.cornell.edu/teaching-ideas/engaging-students/active-learning.html

Active Learning, http://www.studygs.net/activelearn.htm

Tracy, Brian, *Expand Your Mind: Importance Of Lifelong Learning And Continuous Education,* http://www.briantracy.com/blog/personal-success/expand-your-mind-importance-of-lifelong-learning-and-continuous-education/

Reflective Practice: An Approach For Expanding Your Learning Frontiers, http://ocw.mit.edu/courses/urban-studies-and-planning/11-965-reflective-practice-an-approach-for-expanding-your-learning-frontiers-january-iap-2007/

Hansman, Catherine, A, *Context-Based Adult Learning*, https://www.andrews.edu/sed/leadership_dept/documents/context_based_adult_.pdf

Chapter 5

Learning Quotes, http://www.brainyquote.com/quotes/topics/topic_learning.html

What Is A Visual Spacial Learner, http://www.time4learning.com/visual-spatial-learners.shtml

Mann, Rebecca, L, *Eye To Eye: Connecting With Gifted Visual-Spatial Learners (Teaching Strategies)*, http://geri.education.purdue.edu/PDF%20Files/EyeToEye.pdf

Dowd, Mary, Dr, *What Strategies Can I use If I'm An Intrapersonal Learner?* http://everydaylife.globalpost.com/strategies-can-use-im-intrapersonal-learner-15805.html

The Solitary (Intrapersonal) Learning Style, http://www.learning-styles-online.com/style/solitary-intrapersonal/

Auditory Learning: How To Use It To Help Learners Process Information, *http*://www.classroom-management-success.org/auditory-learning.html

The Aural (Auditory-Musical-Rhythmic) Learning Style, http://www.learning-styles-online.com/style/aural-auditory-musical/

Miller, Linda, *Characteristics And Strategies For Different Learning Styles (Intelligences)*, http://www.csus.edu/indiv/p/pfeiferj/edte305/LearningStyle.html

The Social (Interpersonal) Learning Style, http://www.learning-styles-online.com/style/social-interpersonal/

Overview Of Learning Styles, http://artssciences.lamar.edu/_files/documents/nursing/orientation/overview_of_learning_styles.pdf

The Verbal (Linguistic) Learning Style, http://www.learning-styles-online.com/style/verbal-linguistic/

Given, Barbara, K, *Teaching To The Brain's Natural Learning System*, *Chapter 5, The Physical Learning System*, http://www.ascd.org/

publications/books/101075/chapters/The-Physical-Learning-System. aspx

The Logical (Mathematical) Learning Style, http://www.learning-styles-online.com/style/logical-mathematical/

Chapter 6

Mentoring Quotes, http://www.brainyquote.com/quotes/keywords/ mentoring.html

The Value Of Mentoring, http://www.mentoring.org/about_mentor/ value_of_mentoring

Smith, Gregory, P, *The Importance Of Having A Good Mentor*, http:// www.businessknowhow.com/manage/mentor2.htm

Types Of Mentoring Functions, http://www.educause.edu/careers/ special-topic-programs/mentoring/about-mentoring/types-mentoring-functions

Davis, Jodi, The Eight Steps To Developing A Successful Mentoring Partnership, http://www.jodidavis.com/pdfs/8stepsmentoring.pdf

Building Effective Mentoring Partnerships, http://www.pcaddick.com/

The Framework For A Mentoring Process, http://pcaddick.com/page17. html

Cate, Rodney, Dr, *What Does Good Mentoring Look Like?* https://www. ncfr.org/professional-resources/career-resources/students/what-does-good-mentoring-look

Pilon, Annie, *What To Expect And Not To Expect From A Business Mentor*, http://smallbiztrends.com/2014/02/what-to-expect-from-a-business-mentor.html

Jao, Jerry, *Why CEO's Need Mentors – They Accelerate Learning*, http://www.entrepreneur.com/article/239682

Chapter 7

Drive Quotes, http://www.*brainyquote*.com/quotes/keywords/drive. html

Zukav, Gary, *Finding Meaning And Purpose In Your Life*, http://www. oprah.com/spirit/Finding-Meaning-and-Purpose-in-Your-Life

Babauta, Leo, *How To Find Your Life Purpose: An Unconventional Approach*, http://zenhabits.*net*/life-purpose/

Questions That Reveal Your Ultimate Purpose In Life, http://goodlifezen.com/15-questions-that-reveal-your-ultimate-purpose-in-life/

McWhinney, James, *6 Powerful Questions That Will Change Your Life Forever*, http://tinybuddha.com/blog/6-powerful-questions-that-will-change-your-life-forever/

Becker, Joshua, *10 Unconventional Habits To Live Distraction-Less*, http://www.becomingminimalist.com/distraction-less/

10 Ways To Improve Your Personality, http://www.essentiallifeskills.net/improveyourpersonality.html

Kraus, Michael, W, PhD, *The Power To Be Me*, https://www.psychologytoday.com/blog/under-the-influence/201201/the-power-be-me

Chapter 8

Inspire Quotes, http://www.brainyquote.com/quotes/keywords/inspire.html

Ravenscraft, Eric, *The Science Of Inspiration (And How To Make It Work For You)*, http://lifehacker.com/the-science-of-inspiration-and-how-to-make-it-work-for-1467413542

May, Cindi, The Inspiration Paradox: Your Best Creative Time Is Not When You Think, http://www.scientificamerican.com/article/your-best-creative-time-not-when-you-think/

The Ultimate Guide To Motivation – How To Achieve Any Goal, http://zenhabits.net/the-ultimate-guide-to-motivation-how-to-achieve-any-goal/

Clear, James, *The Myth Of Passion And Motivation: How To Stay Focused When You Get Bored Working Toward Your Goals*, https://blog.bufferapp.com/the-myth-of-passion-and-motivation-how-to-stay-focused-when-you-get-bored-working-toward-your-goals

Reynolds, Siimon, *How To Stay Super Motivated*, http://www.forbes.com/sites/siimonreynolds/2013/07/28/how-to-stay-super-motivated/

How To Motivate Yourself To Do Practically Anything, http://well.wvu.
edu/articles/how_to_motivate_yourself_to_do_practically_anything

Tobak, Steve, *How To Be The Best Version Of You,* http://www.inc.
com/steve-tobak/how-to-be-the-best-version-of-you.html

Davenport, Barrie, *25 Ways To Become The Best Version Of Yourself,*
http://liveboldandbloom.com/05/life-coaching/25-ways-to-become-
the-best-version-of-yourself

The Definition Of Greatness, http://elitedaily.com/life/motivation/
definition-greatness/

Chapter 9

Top 10 Take Action Quotes, http://www.movemequotes.com/top-10-
take-action-quotes/

Clear, James, *How Positive Thinking Builds Your Skills, Boosts Your
Health, And Improves Your Work,* http://jamesclear.com/positive-
thinking

Beck, Julie, *How To Build A Happier Brain,* http://www.theatlantic.
com/health/archive/2013/10/how-to-build-a-happier-brain/280752/

Morin, Amy, *10 Tips To Make Positive Thinking Easy,* http://www.
lifehack.org/articles/communication/10-tips-make-positive-thinking-
easy.html

Goleman, Daniel, *Intensity Of Emotion Tied To Perception And
Thinking,* http://www.nytimes.com/1987/03/17/science/intensity-of-
emotion-tied-to-perception-and-thinking.html

*How To Regulate Intense Emotions – Through Grounding, Presence, And
Power Of Choice,* http://www.bellwood.ca/files/articles/How_to_
Regulate_Intense_Emotions_1305554948.pdf

Phases Of Trauma Recovery, http://trauma-recovery.ca/recovery/
phases-of-trauma-recovery/

Smith, Melinda, Segal, Jeanne, *Trauma Stress – The Emotional
Aftermath Of Traumatic Events,* http://www.helpguide.org/articles/
ptsd-trauma/traumatic-stress.htm

Mercola, Joseph, M, 5 Tips For Recovering From Emotional Pain, http://
articles.mercola.com/sites/articles/archive/2013/08/15/emotional-

pain-recovery-.aspx

Chapter 10

Your Dream Quotes, http://www.brainyquote.com/quotes/keywords/your_dreams.html

How To Finally Find The Courage To Pursue Your Dream, https://www.themuse.com/advice/how-to-finally-find-the-courage-to-pursue-your-dream

Hiller, Bernard, *What's Stopping You From Achieving Your Dreams,* http://www.huffingtonpost.com/bernard-hiller-/why-cant-you-achieve-your_b_5980230.html

Burkes, Paige, *Your Attitude Determines Your Outcome,* http://www.simplemindfulness.com/2012/03/25/attitude-determines-outcome/

*How Your Perspective Affects Your Attitude, http://*ownyourambition.com/how-your-perspective-affects-your-attitude/

Moore, Sean, *Consistent Discipline = Personal Growth,* http://medexec.org/consistent-discipline-personal-growth/

Savara, Sid, *The Only Consistent Secret For Personal Growth,* http://sidsavara.com/personal-development/the-only-consistent-secret-for-personal-growth

Maxwell, John, C, *15 Invaluable Laws Of Growth,* http://www.slideshare.net/bright9977/15-invaluable-laws-of-growth-by-john-c-maxwell

Sullivan, Sean, *Consistency Fosters Personal Growth,* http://www.convergestreet.com/consistency-fosters-personal-growth/

Chapter 11

9 Growth Hacking Quotes, https://line.do/9-growth-hacking-quotes/cez/vertical

Bachis, Adam, *A Systematic Approach To Solving Just About Any Problem,* http://lifehacker.com/5795228/how-to-solve-just-about-any-problem

Morin, Amy, *7 Scientifically Proven Benefits Of Gratitude That Will Motivate You To Give Thanks Year-Round,* http://www.forbes.com/

sites/amymorin/2014/11/23/7-scientifically-proven-benefits-of-gratitude-that-will-motivate-you-to-give-thanks-year-round/

Amin, Amit, *The 31 Benefits Of Gratitude You Didn't Know About: How Gratitude Can Change Your Life*, http://happierhuman.com/benefits-of-gratitude/

Problem Solving, http://www.skillsyouneed.com/ips/problem-solving.html

Sonnenberg, Frank, *The Power Of A Positive Attitude*, http://www.franksonnenbergonline.com/blog/the-power-of-a-positive-attitude/

Clear, James, *The Science of Positive Thinking: How Positive Thoughts Build Your Skills, Boost Your Health, and Improve Your Work*, http://www.huffingtonpost.com/james-clear/positive-thinking_b_3512202.html

Chahal, Gurbaksh, *When You Come From Nothing, Anything Is Possible: How I was Able To Live 'The Dream'*, http://elitedaily.com/money/when-you-come-from-nothing-anything-is-possible-how-i-was-able-to-live-the-dream/

McMillan, Tracy, *7 Best Pieces Of Advice For People Who Want To Move Past A Rotten Childhood*, http://www.oprah.com/relationships/7-Best-Pieces-of-Advice-for-People-Who-Want-to-Move-Past-a-Rotten-Childhood

Chapter 12

Personal Growth Quotes, http://www.brainyquote.com/quotes/keywords/personal_growth.html

Hill, Adam, *Stop Abandoning Your Goals! 4 Ways To Turn Dreams Into Reality*, http://www.mindbodygreen.com/0-10876/stop-abandoning-your-goals-4-ways-to-turn-dreams-into-reality.html

Braime, Hannah, *How Writing Things Down Can Change Your Life*, http://www.lifehack.org/articles/lifestyle/how-writing-things-down-can-change-your-life.html

Marshall, Lisa, B, *How To Communicate Better Using The Rule Of Three*, http://www.quickanddirtytips.com/business-career/public-speaking/how-to-communicate-better-using-the-rule-of-three

Gallo, Carmine, *Thomas Jefferson, Steve Jobs, And The Rule Of 3,* http://www.forbes.com/sites/carminegallo/2012/07/02/thomas-jefferson-steve-jobs-and-the-rule-of-3/

Creating A Strategy To Achieve Smart Goals, https://www.webucator.com/tutorial/goal-setting-time-management/creating-strategy-achieve-smart-goals.cfm

Personal Goal Setting, http://www.mindtools.com/page6.html

Robbins, Mike, *Speak Your Truth,* http://www.oprah.com/spirit/Speak-Your-Truth_2

Chapter 13

Excellence Quotes, http://www.brainyquote.com/quotes/keywords/excellence.html

Kaufman, Scott, Barry, *Why Inspiration Matters,* https://hbr.org/2011/11/why-inspiration-matters/

Olsen, Andrew, *Why Inspiring Others Is The Secret To Success,* http://blog.brazencareerist.com/2012/03/27/why-inspiring-others-is-the-secret-to-success/

Seidman, Dov, *The Importance Of Inspirational Leadership,* http://www.fastcompany.com/1294669/importance-inspirational-leadership

Dalai, Lama, *20 Ways To Get Good Karma,* http://www.spiritualnow.com/articles/25/1/20-Ways-to-Get-Good-Karma/Page1.html

La Meaux, E, C, *How To Attract Good Karma,* http://life.gaiam.com/article/how-attract-good-karma

Mallen, Daniel, *The Simplest Ways To Inspire People And Change Their Life,* http://www.lifehack.org/articles/communication/20-ways-inspire-people-around-you.html

Caprino, Kathy, *9 Core Behaviors Of People Who Positively Impact The World,* http://www.forbes.com/sites/kathycaprino/2014/06/02/9-core-behaviors-of-people-who-positively-impact-the-world/

Chapter 14

Excellence Quotes, http://www.brainyquote.com/quotes/keywords/excellence.html

Khan, Salman, *Why Pursue Excellence,* http://www.academia.edu/4091169/Why_pursue_Excellence

Parvin, Cordell, *Are You Pursuing Excellence Or Success,* http://www.cordellblog.com/career-development/are-you-pursuing-excellence-or-success/

Hutchinson, Alex, *Cracking The Athlete's Brain,* http://www.outsideonline.com/fitness/mental-conditioning/Head-Games-Brain-Injuries-Study-Athletes.html

Goodman, Nadia, *How To Stay Focused: Train Your Brain,* http://www.entrepreneur.com/blog/225321

Morgan, John, *Why You Should Share Your Success,* http://johnmichaelmorgan.com/why-you-should-share-your-success/

Notter, Jamie, *Create A Culture That Drives Success, Not One That Makes You Feel Good,* http://blog.clarity.fm/culture-that-drives-success/

Quast, Lisa, *To Get Ahead, Help Develop Others' Careers,* http://www.forbes.com/sites/lisaquast/2012/10/01/to-get-ahead-in-your-career-develop-others/

Is Giving The Secret To Getting Ahead, http://www.nytimes.com/2013/03/31/magazine/is-giving-the-secret-to-getting-ahead.html?pagewanted=all&_r=0

Cuffin, Eddie, *10 Ways To Achieve Success In Both Business And Life,* http://elitedaily.com/money/entrepreneurship/10-ways-to-be-successful-in-business-and-in-life/

Chapter 15

Mentors Quotes, http://www.brainyquote.com/quotes/keywords/mentors.html

The 8 Keys Of Excellence – Definitions And Descriptions, http://www.8keys.org/8keys_defined.aspx

Edberg, Henrik, *Bruce Lee's Top 7 Fundamentals For Getting Your Life In Shape,* http://www.positivityblog.com/index.php/2008/03/07/bruce-lees-top-7-fundamentals-for-getting-your-life-in-shape/

Servant Leadership: Helping People Come Alive, https://www.

psychologytoday.com/blog/pay-it-forward/201207/servant-leadership-helping-people-come-alive

McDowell, Adelle, *Pay It Forward,* http://www.selfgrowth.com/articles/pay-it-forward

Mentoring, An Essential Leadership Skill, http://www.mindtools.com/pages/article/newCDV_70.htm

Morgan, Jacob, *Why The Future Of Work Is All About Challenging Convention,* http://www.forbes.com/sites/jacobmorgan/2014/06/24/the-future-work-challenging-convention/

Deschene, Lori, *8 Ways To Be More Confident: Live The Life Of Yours Dreams,* http://tinybuddha.com/blog/8-ways-to-be-more-confident-live-the-life-of-your-dreams/

ABOUT THE AUTHOR

Iris González was born in Boston, MA, and received her Bachelor's degree in Engineering from Smith College. She started her career as a Project Manager in Information Technology, and in July 2014 she moved to Miami, FL, to pursue her dreams as an engineer. With a strong desire to "pay it forward" and help others, she started her own business at the age of 25 that is dedicated to empowering individuals to unleash their inner warrior and build out their vision.

Iris is a sought after public speaker and workshop leader who teaches and travels throughout the world. She uses her story as a means to inspire "at-risk" youth to stay strong and is a strong advocate for mentoring.

Made in the USA
San Bernardino, CA
05 April 2015